THE NOTARY BUSINESS BUILDING CHALLENGE

90 DAYS TO MORE CLIENTS, MORE INCOME, AND MORE CONFIDENCE

BY BILL SOROKA

The Notary Business Building Challenge: 90 Days to More Clients, More Income, and More Confidence

First Edition

Editor: Beverly Lickteig Loder

Book Layout and Design: Tracy Atkins (TheBookMakers.com)

Cover Design: Tanja Prokop

ISBN 9798354700851 (Paperback)

http://www.NotaryCoach.com

Find Free Resources and Tools on the
Readers Resource Website at:

www.NotaryCoach.com/90

CONTENTS

fluff, no more disappointment . . . and no more teasing just for a chance to upsell you into the "good" package.

We included everything you need to succeed in one price. Here's what's included:

- The full Sign & Thrive Notary Training Course and Community for loan signing work by Bill Soroka

- Full access to Laura Biewer Presents . . . Training and Replay Library for General & Specialty Notary Work

- The replays to *every* state included in Laura's Real World Notary Training

- Full Access to the entire Signing Agent Marketing (SAM) program for direct-escrow work by Jennifer Neitzel

- The full Apostille Agent Masterclass and Certification Program from Lawrence Institute for Notaries by Judi Lawrence

- The LinkedIn Professional Profile Course for personal branding online by Sandra Long

- The Get Known Strategy for Online Content Creation and Email/Social Media Distribution by Zion Brock

- The First Page SEO for Notaries course to teach Search Engine Optimization by Tyler Botsford

- Google Business Profile Content Creation by Jim Allen, the Marketing Notary

- Over 20 live teaching calls with these instructors (and more) every single month for more in-depth and detailed training

- The TOMM app for prospecting and staying in touch with your network

- NotaryAssist bookkeeping software

It's all included. One monthly price. Cancel anytime. If you're craving open-hearted Notaries who share their wins, strategies, and challenges in an open forum, plus the wisdom of great teachers and fellow Notary entrepreneurs, then NBB is for you.

Don't make me beg (because I will—that's how sure I am that NBB can help).

Just join us at www.NotaryCoach.com/nbbfresh.

This business, as a mobile Notary and loan signing agent, has the power to change lives. Yours, your family's, and your clients'. You deserve it.

Before you begin the challenge, allow me to share a little more about the opportunity at hand with what I call "the Notary Funnel."

THE NOTARY FUNNEL

"The Notary Funnel" is a concept I created a few years ago as I formulated a way to enhance my client's experience with me. I knew there had to be a better way to not only find new customers, but retain them longer than just one appointment. Why couldn't I stay in touch with my signers and keep myself top of mind so that when they needed a Notary again, they'd think of me?

As I created my own personal "Top of Mind Method," it became clear there were opportunities to connect more deeply with my customers/signers as they moved through my business as a Notary Public and loan signing agent. I called it the Notary Funnel.

The Notary Funnel is your customer's journey through your business and brand. That's it. Simple yet powerful.

Whether you are a

- mobile Notary,

- loan signing agent,

- apostille agent,

- wedding officiant,

- fingerprint technician,

- field inspector,

or anything else under the Notary umbrella or beyond, understanding the impact of the Notary Funnel will help you build a business that lasts, no matter what.

Picture the wide mouth of a typical funnel. This is how your customers come into your business. They pour in from all your efforts cultivating relationships and optimizing your digital presence.

Think about all those sources of business:

- Website

- Online directories

- Blogs

- Vlogs
- Google Business Profile
- Google Ads
- Social media
- Networking meetings
- Current clients
- Real estate agents
- Loan officers
- Attorneys
- Friends
- Family
- Client-getting events

It all boils down to two sources: Technology and People. We bust our humps finding new customers to bring into our funnel. But then what?

Most Notaries have a funnel that looks like this:

After working hard to get your phone to ring and ding, the customer calls, you take care of them, and that's that. If you're lucky they save your number in their phone and remember to call you the next time they need a Notary.

If you're lucky.

This "one-time use" paradigm for Notaries isn't necessarily your fault. Our culture has conspired to devalue the importance of a Notary, and frankly, most people don't even know what it is we do.

That's why it's our responsibility, and our great opportunity, to educate the public and even give them permission to expect a different relationship with their Notary. This can be, and in fact *is*, much more than simply signing, dating, and stamping a piece of paper.

What we have here is the potential for something much, much, bigger.

The Lifetime Value of Customer Relationships

The truth is, the instant we move from this transactional thinking to transformational thinking, as my friend Jen Neitzel puts it, our business changes completely.

It's easy to fall into the trap of valuing each appointment as *only* the fee that we get to collect.

- $25 for this car title transfer
- $150 for this refinance
- $200 for this Living Trust
- $300 for this home purchase
- $20 for this Minor Travel Consent Form

Consider this: If they needed a Notary once, they'll need one again. And even if they don't need you again, they'll likely know someone else who needs a great Notary.

Over a couple of years, prime clients can be worth $1,500 to $2,500 in fees if they're involved in commerce and travel internationally, have children, or are simply employed.

And guess what? They probably have friends who do the same. Your referrals are gold in these circles.

The lifetime value of your customers is far more than the initial fee for your service.

And this is just the extrinsic value of your customer relationships. This usually gets the most attention because it's how we pay our bills and what we're trained to talk about:

- Revenue/money

- Profits

- Status/prestige

There's nothing wrong with extrinsic results. In business, this is how we distinguish between a business and a hobby. No revenue . . . no business. We need customers and we need revenue.

But there's more to building a business we can be proud of. There's the intrinsic side of the value of customer relationships as well, meaning things such as

- Joy

- Sense of meaning and purpose

- Confidence

And while I love the freedom and options money brings to my life, it's secondary to these intrinsic factors. This stuff is important. And what a gift that you and I get a chance at experiencing it in this business.

But it's not just about us. We have customers, too, and they're having their own experiences. They have their own perception of the value of our relationship, both extrinsic and intrinsic.

When I look back at my appointments, I can get a clear picture of the extrinsic value my clients get out of our transaction:

- Cash out from a refi for whatever they need or want

- Lower interest rates and lower payments leave more cash in their pockets

- Investment property to build a legacy

- First-time home ownership

- Peace of mind having affairs in order

- Buying/selling dream vehicles

When my business truly started to thrive, though, was after I started to realize the intrinsic side of their experience, too.

Sure, my customers had a need and an objective. They had a problem—they needed something called a Notary to stamp a document so they could get what they wanted. But they're also human beings with similar needs to me and to the rest of us—the quest for joy, connection, and purpose.

What if I was a beacon of love and light at my appointments? What if, in addition to my expertise and my stamp, I also brought some humanity and an invitation for something more?

What if I could bring

- Joy

- Connection

- Meaning and purpose

to each of my appointments?

What evolved from that realization is that the Notary Funnel doesn't have to be the stunted example I showed previously.

Your customers don't have to drop like a rock into a pit of forgotten despair after your initial service appointment.

We can actually extend the "tube" a bit, slowing the customer journey so they can get to know, like, and trust us a bit.

There are different "touch" or connection points throughout the entire funnel—thirteen of them, to be exact. A collection of opportunities I call "the Top of Mind Method."

THE TOP OF MIND METHOD
THROUGH THE NOTARY FUNNEL:

Opportunity #1: Response and Close

Simply said, this is your "first impression" with potential customers. Do you answer the phone? *How* do you answer the phone? And, do you have the systems in place to communicate effectively when you can't answer the phone? This opportunity goes a bit further too. How well do you overcome price objections, demonstrate your expertise, build a rapport, and actually book the appointment?

Opportunity #2: Expert Delivery of Your Services

If you sealed the deal in Opportunity #1 and got the appointment, remember you've been hired for a job, and an important one at that. Whether your client knows it or not, they want an expert Notary who knows what they can do . . . and what they can't. That ensures there will be no problems in the future. What steps do you take to elevate yourself to expert status?

Opportunity #3: Lay the Foundation for a Relationship That Can Last

When you show up fully present to an appointment and put people over paper, taking care to make eye contact and follow social cues for humor, empathy, and compassion, you can open the door to deeper and longer-term relationships.

Opportunity #4: Ask Permission to Stay in Touch

When you've successfully implemented Opportunities 1–3, asking permission to stay in touch is easy. In fact, when done correctly, you'll be laughing (or crying) with your customers like old friends at the signing table. It's almost weird *not* to stay in touch. I have a 100% success rate with this opportunity because I found a smooth way to ask *only* the people I like and *want* to stay in touch with. Why? Because the feeling is mutual! You like them, they like you, so stay in touch and keep yourself *top of mind*.

Opportunity #5: Button Up Your Appointment

Maybe I should have named this opportunity the "Gain Peace of Mind," because that's exactly what will happen when you have a solid *post-appointment ritual*. A ritual is simply a string of habits. So, after every single appointment, what do you do? For me, while I'm in the car (usually parked around the corner from the appointment or at a coffee shop), I do 3 to 5 things right away. For you, maybe it's some of these:

- Send the invoice.

- Send a thank-you card or email (or both).

- Update hiring company.

- Scan documents.

- Send a text asking for a review.

- Update your CRM (Customer Relationship Management software).

- And, importantly, update your bookkeeping.

One of the big mistakes we make as solo-preneurs is to say that we "will do it later." While that is sometimes true, "later" usually comes with much more stress than necessary (think tax time). Give yourself the gift of peace of mind and set up your own post-appointment ritual.

Opportunity #6: Use Email to Stay in Touch Occasionally

Have you looked at your inbox lately? Every business in the world uses email to bring value to their customers. Sometimes it's in the form of coupons or discounts. Sometimes it's more information or tools to help you use their product or improve your business or life. And, sure, some people and companies do this better than others. We're not talking about spam here; we're talking about genuine communications that aim to bring value to customers. As a Notary you can do this by demonstrating your expertise on topics, sharing information, or simply reminding your past, previous, and prospective clients that your services exist (we have lots of room for growth here!).

As you battle with all the resistance to this opportunity going on in your head right now, keep this in mind: Businesses don't continue to send emails because they *don't* work. They send them because they DO work.

Opportunity #7: Broadcast More Value

In this modern age, it's relatively easy to create content your *customers* may find helpful. After all, they aren't used to paperwork and details and all the processes surrounding mortgages, trusts, apostilles, etc. They need your expert guidance. You can create videos (vlogs), blogs, articles, and even simple social media posts that help your customers navigate any number of situations in life. Or, you can simply share your journey. People *love* passion.

When you're passionate about what you do, share your day-to-day. Then use modern technology, social media platforms, and email to broadcast that content to your audience.

Opportunity #8: Engage with Other's Content

Your ideal client has a dream of their own, and whether that is an attorney, an escrow officer, or a hospital administrator, they are likely creating their own content (because it works). Get in their orbit and *thoughtfully* like, comment on, and share their content with your audience.

Opportunity #9: Reach Out to Your Network

Once your customers slowly wind through the funnel of your business, they've been given a chance to see what you're all about—a chance to get to *know* you, *trust* you, and maybe even *like* you. Those are important elements of a relationship, yes?

With this opportunity, you get a chance to "deepify" that relationship by reaching out to a client (or a few) each day to let them know you care and are thinking about them. We do this all the time with friends and family, and it's absolutely okay to do with business contacts too. It's actually quite simple, and we, of course, tend to overthink it.

Opportunity #10: Send a Handwritten Note

Sending notes and cards changed my business *and my life*. To your customer, there is something special about receiving a simple, thoughtful message from you written by hand. Especially if it does *not* include your business card or any business branding that would make it an advertising piece, NOT a connection piece. Something incredibly powerful also happens for you when you include doing a random act of kindness, or shall I say an *intentional* act of kindness, such as sending a handwritten note in your daily activities.

If you did only Opportunities #9 and #10 every single day for the rest of your life, you'd never want for a customer again.

Opportunity #11: Be a Resource to Your Network

Your network is bigger than you realize. For some reason, we always underestimate that. Think of all your social media, email, and phone contacts. The people you work with, train with, or went to school with. All in your network. And they all need something sometime. The more you are the connector for those who need something with those who have that something, the more valuable you become to your network. It doesn't have to be *just* your Notary services. It can be recommending your favorite preschool, your favorite breakfast burrito (yum!), or the handyman who power-washed your house last year. You have people and companies you love to work with; introduce them to your network as appropriate.

Opportunity #12: Expand Your Peer Network

Notaries need Notaries too. Not just for documents, but for support. This business isn't easy. Clients are not always rainbows and unicorns. Sometimes you need to talk to someone who just gets it. Your peer network of Notaries can be your partners in growth through sharing information, strategies, and yes, even customers. Good Notaries like to partner with other good Notaries. Get dialed into live conference events, online events and training, or local Notary meet-up groups (yes, they exist, but if they don't near you, consider starting one!).

Opportunity #13: Attend Client-Getting Events

With clarity comes clients. When you are crystal clear on who your ideal customer is, you can find out where they congregate. Attorneys (every specialization), escrow officers, and even hospital administrators have association meetings, conventions, conferences, or training programs that you can attend, sponsor, or otherwise support. Attend five client-getting events each year, connect on a deeper level, and invite them into your funnel so they too get a chance to know, like, and trust you.

So there you have it: the Notary Funnel that represents your customer's journey through your business and the Top of Mind Method with its 13 opportunities to connect on a deeper level.

Your new Notary Funnel looks like this:

Opportunity #1: Response and Close
Opportunity #2: Expert Delivery of Your Services
Opportunity #3: Lay the Foundation for a Relationship That Can Last
Opportunity #4: Ask Permission to Stay in Touch
Opportunity #5: Button Up Your Appointment
Opportunity #6: Use Email to Stay in Touch Occasionally
Opportunity #7: Broadcast More Value
Opportunity #8: Engage with Other's Content
Opportunity #9: Reach Out to Your Network
Opportunity #10: Send a Handwritten Note
Opportunity #11: Be a Resource to Your Network
Opportunity #12: Expand Your Peer Network
Opportunity #13: Attend Client-Getting Events

This Notary Funnel is unconventional because both parties, signer and Notary, have been trained for immediate gratification, the one-and-done philosophy. But you can change that, starting today.

This 90-Day Notary Business Building Challenge is designed to help.

Every day you'll be given a lesson and a challenge that will either bring more prospects into your funnel OR help you cultivate deeper relationships with them once they're in there.

And now we begin the Notary Business Building Challenge . . .

DAY 1
GOOGLE "NOTARY NEAR ME"

Have you ever Googled yourself?

I'd like you to do it now . . . kind of.

Pull up the most popular search engine in the world right now, Google, and type in "Notary Near Me" (no quotes).

If you really want to get some honest results, do this from the "Incognito" browser feature in Chrome. Doing so allows the browser to "forget" your previous browsing history, cookies, and biases and pull up true organic results. (For a video on how to search with an incognito tab, please visit the Readers Resource Website for this book at www.NotaryCoach.com/90.)

Please note: Do NOT Google your personal name or business name for the sake of this exercise. Your prospects aren't going to search for you by name because they either won't know it yet, or they won't remember it.

As you progress in business, consider your customer's journey and you'll see the potholes and bumps in the road they encounter. Look at your results from this search—the same results your prospects get. How do they decide who to call? What happens when they call?

This industry is *ripe* for innovation and those with the courage to be the innovator. What opportunities do you see to help yourself stand out in the sea of sameness?

People don't need a Notary until they need a Notary; that's the nature of our business.

Your job, then, is to make it easy to find you when they need you.

Once you see where you stand in Google rankings, you have your benchmark. Are you in the top three listings? Are you on page one? Page 100?

Don't be ashamed of where you end up! We're here to learn. This knowledge will help you gauge your search engine optimization (SEO) efforts moving forward.

Date Completed:

Challenge Review

Notes or initial observations:

What worked:

What didn't work:

What will you continue to do?

What will you do differently next time?

DAY 2
MAKE A "NOTE-WRITING KIT"

Sending handwritten notes can be life-changing. And not just for the recipient, but for you!

There's a special magic to including this intentional act of kindness as part of your workday.

I've found that most people often wish they sent more handwritten notes and cards. But life gets in the way:

- You have to buy stationery or cards.

- Then envelopes.

- And stamps.

- Then you actually have to find time to write the note . . . and mail it.

This works a lot easier if you set yourself up for success.

For Day Two of your Notary Funnel Challenge, put together your own Note-Writing Kit.

Here's what you need:

- Stationery or cards (can be plain, unbranded, or even fancier with a monogram, etc.)

- Envelopes

- Pen

- Stamps

- Container to hold everything

That's it!

Then, schedule a time to write someone a note each day. A friend. Colleague. Client. Prospect. You name it!

This should be unbranded—no business cards allowed.

It's a simple connection to let people know you're thinking of them.

Even a message as simple as, "Hi Susan, I was thinking about you the other day. Wishing you well! –Bill (The Notary)"

If you don't see yourself as handwriting and mailing traditional-style notes and cards, there are some online options for creating and sending printed cards too. SendOutCards (SOC) is a favorite resource of mine because I can customize the card fronts with photos from appointments (taken with permission, of course). Customers *love* seeing pictures of their pets! SOC also allows you to upload a sample of your own handwriting so when the cards are printed, the font resembles your own writing.

Enjoy your note-writing adventures!

Date Completed:

Challenge Review

Notes or initial observations:

What worked:

What didn't work:

What will you continue to do?

What will you do differently next time?

DAY 3
LIST FIVE PEOPLE TO CONTACT THIS WEEK

Today I have an easy challenge for you.

Take out a piece of paper—or whatever you use to take notes—and list the names of five people you can reach out to this week.

These don't have to be business-related contacts. You can include old friends or even family members you haven't checked in with for awhile.

Here's the thing: You haven't checked in with them lately so . . . they may not be top of mind for you right now, and that's okay. Scroll through your phone contacts and see who pops out at you. Follow the promptings. Write down at least five of those names.

That's it. That's the end of the challenge today!

But . . .

Chances are, you're not here in the Notary Funnel Challenge because you just want to scrape by doing the bare minimum, right?

I didn't think so.

Take today's challenge to the next level a few different ways:

1. Commit to reaching out to ONE PERSON from your list each day this week.

2. Schedule it on your calendar.

3. Do this every day from now on.

I am convinced that every one of us already knows exactly whom we need to know to scale our business to the levels we dream of. We simply lose touch and connection with them as life happens.

This exercise is the remedy to that.

Challenge Review

Notes or initial observations:

What worked:

What didn't work:

What will you continue to do?

What will you do differently next time?

DAY 4
LEAVE A POSITIVE REVIEW FOR THE LAST BUSINESS OR SERVICE YOU ENJOYED

It's been estimated that 9 out of 10 consumers are influenced by reviews before they make a purchasing decision or choose a restaurant.

Authentic reviews can make or break a business.

And yet, only about 10% of consumers actually take the time to write an online review.

Look at the influence that 10% have over the rest of us!

In today's challenge, we're going to do our part to balance those scales a bit, and hopefully make a positive difference for a small business that needs you.

Think about some of your recent expenditures:

- Coffee
- Groceries
- Landscaping
- Art
- Music (album)
- Book
- Events
- Breakfast burrito
- Dining experience
- Handyman service
- Hotel
- Apartment community
- Refinance (Loan Officer)

- Whatever—No limits

Choose one business that stands out for providing a great experience and find them online with a quick Google search. If they've set up their Google Business Profile, this will be super easy and you can quickly find the RE-VIEWS section and add your own.

If the business you are trying to support doesn't have their Google Business Profile set up yet, you may have to search a little further to leave a review. Do they have a Yelp profile? Or maybe a Facebook or LinkedIn profile?

Since this is a part of the challenge, and you've already set this time aside today, take the few extra minutes to track down the best location to write a review. If you still can't find one, send them a complimentary email via the Contact page on their website, or by some other means. Let them know you've been looking everywhere for a place to post a positive five-star review, because you want the world to know how much you enjoyed your experience.

Easy peasy.

Spread some joy and support a small business.

Want to take this to the next level?

Make a habit of this.

If you experience some goodness, share it with the rest of us, and support a fellow entrepreneur at the same time.

Date Completed:

Challenge Review

Notes or initial observations:

What worked:

What didn't work:

What will you continue to do?

What will you do differently next time?

DAY 5
OPTIMIZE BOOKKEEPING

Do you dread tax time?

Each year many small business owners, especially Notaries, end up stressing out more and more as April 15 approaches.

Why?

Many of us fall into the trap of believing we are superhuman.

We actually believe that on top of facilitating multiple appointments throughout the day, doing our marketing, answering inquiries, getting the kids off to school, folding laundry, meeting up with friends, snuggling up to *Bridgerton*, walking the dogs, and making dinner, we're actually going to sit down each night and input the day's transactions, expenses, and receipts into an Excel spreadsheet that we'll decipher on April 14.

There are a few "unicorns" out there who do this brilliantly; you know who you are.

But the rest of us?

We need HELP!

This is where systems and tools can pave the way for you.

Today's challenge is to choose a bookkeeping program that will work the way your mind does.

If you're good at Excel, use it.

If you know QuickBooks, use it.

If you want Notary-specific software that understands our way of doing business, here are two to try (find links on the Readers Resource Website at www.NotaryCoach.com/90):

- NotaryAssist (included with NBB membership)

- NotaryGadget

Then, take this challenge to the next level by including bookkeeping as part of your "post-appointment ritual." This consists of four or five things that you can do after every appointment that help ensure what must get done actually does get done.

Here are some ideas for your post-appointment ritual:

- Wrap up bookkeeping.

- Send an invoice.

- Check your documents—again.

- Send a thank-you note by email or text and request a review.

It's your business! You can build your post-appointment ritual any way that serves you and your customers best.

The key is to build a bookkeeping habit that supports your peace of mind so you can focus on client acquisition and revenue-producing activities.

Date Completed:

Challenge Review

Notes or initial observations:

What worked:

What didn't work:

What will you continue to do?

What will you do differently next time?

DAY 6
CLARIFY YOUR AFFIRMATIONS

I have fallen in and out of love with the idea of positive affirmations several times in my life.

I am back in love with them now, by the way.

Who wouldn't like the idea of saying nice things to yourself?

I don't know about you, but my inner critic can be a real bi-, uh, jerk, sometimes. Hearing something nice and empowering every now and again would be a welcome change.

But we can't just stick a Post-it on the mirror and recite, "I'm good enough, I'm smart enough, and doggone it, people like me" once a day and then turn the reins back over to that overbearing inner critic.

We have to choose affirmations that matter to us. And we have to remind ourselves of them throughout the day.

That's your challenge here for Day Six of the Notary Funnel Challenge:

1. Find or create an affirmation that lights YOU up. You don't have to explain it to anyone else. It's yours, and it's as private as you want to keep it.

2. Start your day with your new affirmation. There's something about reading it out loud that greatly enhances this, but if you aren't ready for that, just read it, enthusiastically, to yourself in the morning.

3. Set three alarms on your smartphone to remind you to read your affirmation again throughout the day when the alarm rings. On modern smartphones, you can actually label the alarm with the actual text of your affirmation if you want.

There are a lot of empowering words and phrases out there, and you'll be tempted to choose more than one affirmation. While there are no rules to this game of life, I recommend you start this new system with ONE affirmation that brings you into laser focus on one of your primary goals. You can always add more later.

Affirmations can change as your priorities change. This is a fluid activity.

Need some ideas for affirmations? I've shared some of my favorites I've used throughout the years below. In addition, you can Google "Positive affirmation ideas" and get over a million pages of ideas. I've also found that a good quote can sometimes do the trick.

1. **My favorite affirmations:** Speaking of quotes, while creating my course and writing my first book I recited Theodore Roosevelt's "The Man in the Arena" speech out loud in the shower each morning to help me overcome my inner critic's question of "Who do you think you are?" Are you doing big things too? **See if this moves you** (understanding, of course, that "woman" is interchangeable with "man" throughout):

"It is not the critic who counts; not the man who points out how the strong man stumbles, or where the doer of deeds could have done them better. The credit belongs to the man who is actually in the arena, whose face is marred by dust and sweat and blood; who strives valiantly; who errs, who comes short again and again, because there is no effort without error and shortcoming; but who does actually strive to do the deeds; who knows great enthusiasms, the great devotions; who spends himself in a worthy cause; who at the best knows in the end the triumph of high achievement, and who at the worst, if he fails, at least fails while daring greatly, so that his place shall never be with those cold and timid souls who neither know victory nor defeat."

2. TODAY, I CHOOSE GREATNESS. I don't care how I feel. I am a person of my word and I will do what I said I would do. I will honor my word, especially to myself.

3. I act in accordance with my highest and best self at all times.

4. Every day is an adventure.

5. Each and every day, someone, somewhere in this city, needs my services. My job TODAY is to find that person.

6. Every day, I take action to build my dreams. I do not let the sun set without taking a step toward my goals.

7. I am in flow with the universe and love, opportunities, and money flow abundantly into my life.

8. I LOVE networking and I look forward to meeting new people every day.

9. I am a valuable resource to people and they reach out to me with their needs.

10. This too shall pass. No struggle, no progress.

Use whatever energizes you and keeps you moving, especially when things get tough.

Your headspace is just about the only thing you have any control over. Affirmations can help you design that internal support structure.

I share even more affirmations and exactly how I use them in my Morning Mastery Course. For a video on where to find it in the NBB program content, visit the Reader's Resource Website at www.NotaryCoach.com/90.

Date Completed:

Challenge Review

Notes or initial observations:

What worked:

What didn't work:

What will you continue to do?

What will you do differently next time?

DAY 7
CREATE A CONFIRMATION VIDEO

Ready to try something new?

The Day 7 Challenge is going to stretch your comfort zone.

Today, consider creating a brief prerecorded confirmation video to send out to signers just prior to your scheduled appointments.

You can use this video to

- Set COVID-19 protocol.

- Advise of potential time frame.

- Explain your guidelines and procedures, space requirements, and other suggestions for appointments.

- Inform of ID requirements.

Real quick, watch a sample confirmation video on the Readers Resource Website at www.NotaryCoach.com/90.

Recording a video on your phone is best. As you can see from my example, you don't have to be perfect. Just be you and convey the information clearly and succinctly.

Here are some things to keep in mind for your video:

- Draft an outline first with your main points to convey.

- Keep the length under a minute (ideally).

- Practice it a few times.

- Look directly into the lens (not at yourself) when you record.

- Consider creating different videos for various appointment types if necessary.

Videos like these help build rapport with your signers long before you ring their doorbell, allowing them to get to know you, like you, and trust you. It also sets you apart from nearly every other Notary in the world.

And aren't you looking for a way to differentiate yourself?

If you need a place to host your videos, YouTube (unlimited space) and Google Drive (limited space) offer this for free. You can upload your videos as "unlisted" or "private" and no one will see them unless they have the link, which you can text or email.

Date Completed:

Challenge Review

Notes or initial observations:

What worked:

What didn't work:

What will you continue to do?

What will you do differently next time?

DAY 8
CREATE A HIERARCHY OF SUPPORT

Part of being a Notary "expert" is knowing where to find the answers you need.

You don't necessarily have to know all the answers off the top of your head.

Just be resourceful and self-reliant like MacGyver!

To help keep clarity on exactly what those resources are for you, I encourage you to create a "Hierarchy of Support." This is simply a list of options to prompt you when the pressure is on at an appointment or just before an appointment when you have a pressing concern.

It doesn't have to be anything fancy.

Just handwrite it or type it onto a piece of paper and tape it to the inside cover of your Notary journal or your daily planner (or whatever you carry with you to appointments, e.g., clipboard, etc.). And, permission to laminate your list is granted. I love a good lamination opportunity.

Your list might look like this:

Hierarchy of Support

- State Statutes or Notary Handbook issued by State (always keep accessible to consult first for an answer)

- *U.S. Notary Primer* (and carry this with you)

- Secretary of State Office (include ph. #)

- National Notary Association (NNA) Member Hotline (include ph. #)

- Trusted mentor #1 (include ph. #)

- Trusted mentor #2 (include ph. #)

- Trusted peer group support

- Training resources/classes

- Hiring agency

You can put these avenues of support in any order you want and add or delete from the list, too.

There's something empowering about being able to actually see in writing all the different resources for information and support you have when you're out in the field.

See, just because you're in business for yourself, it doesn't mean you have to be in business *by* yourself.

Date Completed:

Challenge Review

Notes or initial observations:

What worked:

What didn't work:

What will you continue to do?

What will you do differently next time?

DAY 9
START YOUR FAB 100 LIST

Who do you want to do business with?

On the loan signing side of the business, it's easy to fall into the same old tracks we hear on YouTube or Clubhouse all day—Signing Services and Closing Agents. And, there's nothing wrong with that IF it fits your vision and gets you the results you desire.

But this industry is changing.

There's still plenty of business out there. It just looks different than it has the last few years.

Now is the time to dream big.

Pan up a bit, from a soaring eagle's perspective: There's opportunity as far as the eye can see . . . and beyond.

If you could work with anyone, or any company, whom would you choose?

That's your Day 9 Notary Funnel Challenge: Create your Dream 100 list. I call it my Fab 100.

These are the people and brands you WANT to do business with.

Today, start a spreadsheet, or grab a piece of paper, and start writing down names. Yup, start with names only (unless you have contact info handy; then you can add that too).

Start with your own network first. Who do you know that is successful, fun, or respected?

You don't have to do any vetting right now. You don't necessarily need to understand all the hows and whys yet. Just write their names on this list.

Go through your phone or social media if it helps. Maybe even a yearbook.

Once you've gone through your personal network, pay attention to your local community. Whose face is on the bus or the train advertisements? Who has a display ad on the grocery cart?

Listen to the radio. What or whom do you hear on commercial break or as experts in talk radio segments?

I did this with new home construction developments in Phoenix. These new communities spring up everywhere. Who are the builders? Do you want to work with them? Add them to your Fab 100 list.

It's called the Fab 100 for a reason. Strive for 100 names on this list, and keep adding as you encounter new people or new ideas. This list is your go-to in those moments when you're bored or stressed because the phone isn't ringing and you don't know what to do.

This is your Prospect List—a constant stream of possibilities IF you continually cultivate relationships with the people on it. Always remember that while soaring and dreaming big is important, the eagle only eats when he's back down on earth, doing the work.

Later in the NBBC, I'll give you some strategies to help connect deeper with people on this list.

Date Completed:

Challenge Review

Notes or initial observations:

What worked:

What didn't work:

What will you continue to do?

What will you do differently next time?

DAY 10
TAKE A NEW HEADSHOT SELFIE

Let's take a selfie!

Okay, okay, it doesn't have to be a selfie. Someone else could take a picture of you, of course. But with a selfie, you have no excuses. No schedules (or stars) to align. No special equipment. And no special location necessary.

It's all you.

And your online profile pictures make a difference when you're in business.

Yes, you need one.

No, it cannot be your pet, or your logo (you know who you are).

In today's Notary Funnel Challenge, you're going to take a fresh selfie that can be used as your profile picture on social media platforms, online directories, and more.

Tools needed: Smartphone with a camera.

Tips for Taking a Great Headshot:

- Stand/sit up straight with good posture.

- Keep the phone level with your eyes, or just slightly higher (not over your head).

- Play with the angles a bit to find the most flattering for you.

- Take LOTS of pictures so you have some to choose from.

- Change your expression a bit too. Try some smiling, some without. Smiling in a headshot for business is usually recommended, but your style may be different.

- Be sure the lighting is great. If you have access to natural lighting, this can be best. If not, use what you have (and ask your loved ones for feedback if necessary).

- Use a plain background, or at least not one that's distracting. YOU are the main topic.

- Using a tripod OR a friend can be easier when shooting photos, but not required. Full-on arm-length selfies are okay. You can crop your arm out, if necessary.

Once you've identified a few of your favorites, it's time to update your social profiles. It's okay to vary your headshots; you don't have to use the same one for every profile. Just be sure it is clearly you in each photo.

Do this on occasion throughout the year. This keeps your profiles fresh and opens up opportunities for engagement.

Date Completed:

Challenge Review

Notes or initial observations:

What worked:

What didn't work:

What will you continue to do?

What will you do differently next time?

DAY 11
CREATE A LINKEDIN PROFILE

If you're not on LinkedIn yet, today's the day to make it happen.

No more excuses. No more intimidation. You ARE a small business owner and you deserve to be there.

In fact, you're *expected* to be there.

That's where just about everyone you may consider to be your ideal customer is, so yep—you need to be there.

The Day 11 NFC challenge is to create your LinkedIn Profile (if you don't have one).

Start simple and small.

Don't overthink it . . . yet.

Just start.

Join LinkedIn at www.LinkedIn.com. If you want some guidance on this, including step-by-step instructions on how to optimize your profile as you grow your Notary business, Sandra Long and I wrote a book about this called *Supercharge Your Notary Business with LinkedIn*. It can serve as a helpful resource to you.

Already on LinkedIn? Take a look at your profile and make any updates you need to make. New services? New headline? Graphics? There's always a way to enhance your profile.

Supercharge Your Notary Business with LinkedIn is available on my website at www.NotaryCoach.com/books or on Amazon. You'll also find a link to this book on the Readers Resource Website at www.NotaryCoach.com/90, along with a direct link to my LinkedIn profile that you can access so we can connect.

See you on LinkedIn!

Challenge Review

Notes or initial observations:

What worked:

What didn't work:

What will you continue to do?

What will you do differently next time?

DAY 12
USE A LOCAL PHONE NUMBER

Did you know the phone number you use in your online listings and profiles could adversely impact your Google rankings?

It doesn't happen all the time, or under every circumstance, but I think it's important that you know the information that could jam things up for you. After all, you're working hard to boost SEO and your Google rankings so customers can find you. Why let something as small as an area code mess things up?

Google's job is to match those who need stuff/services/info with those who have stuff/services/info. This is called relevance.

In local searches, such as "Notary Near Me," Google likes to be extra sure they match Notaries with consumers who reside in the same area. Part of the way they'll do that is by analyzing phone numbers. That's why it's important to use a phone number with the area code of the city you'll be servicing and where you're building a presence.

But don't get all upset or stressed out if you're not using a local number right now. There are a few reasons to do that these days, such as when you move and want to keep your old number or when new area codes are created and assigned.

For today's challenge, review the tips below and make adjustments to your business phone number as needed:

- You can redirect (forward) a local number obtained through Google Voice (or other services) to any phone number you choose. This means you can list a local number while keeping your current phone number, even if it has an out of state, or out of city, area code.

- In most instances for local services like ours, toll-free numbers may be perceived as antiquated and a turn-off to our customers . . . and to Google! And Google reigns supreme right now. So use a local number instead!

Evaluate your position and your current Google results. Adjust accordingly.

Challenge Review

Notes or initial observations:

What worked:

What didn't work:

What will you continue to do?

What will you do differently next time?

DAY 13
EVALUATE YOUR PAPER BUSINESS CARD

Do me a favor and pull out your business card.

Maybe it's the same card you started this business with.

Maybe it's already gone through a few iterations.

Your challenge for today is to take a fresh, hard look at it and answer these two questions:

- Do you feel proud to hand it out?

- Does it list all the specific info you want to convey?

If the answer to both questions is yes, then congratulations, my friend; your task today is done. Check your supply, order more if necessary, and move along.

But . . .

If the answer to either question is no, then let's go a bit deeper.

I know we like to get all fancy with digital business cards, and ring fobs, and laser doodads—and that is totally fine. I've learned in this business, though, that good old-fashioned business cards are still the gold standard. So, it's beneficial to have a nice business card you can be proud to hand out.

Here are a few tips for (re)designing your business card, as needed:

- Keep it clean and simple (unless you have an eye for design or a template). White space on a card is actually a good thing; it enhances readability.

- Include your name and functional title. A descriptive title will tell people what you do. One good example in our world would be "Mobile Notary and Loan Signing Agent."

- Let the card reflect your personal brand and authentic self. This can be accomplished through your tagline, title, image, logo, etc.

- List all your contact information (obviously!), including preferred phone number, text number, business email address, etc.

- Include a QR code linked to your booking calendar. Okay, this is next level, but it works!

List your website/domain address. Even if you don't have a website per se, get a custom domain that points to your Google Business Profile, LinkedIn profile, SigningAgent.com profile, or similar.

- It can serve you well to include your specialty niches as well. Consider the appointments you either LOVE to perform or make the most income by performing.

- And, if you have a solid digital presence and want to attract followers, include your primary social media handle, e.g., for LinkedIn.

I have two favorite sources for designing and printing business cards: Canva.com and VistaPrint.com. You can both design and print using either individual site, or you can design on Canva and upload to VistaPrint to take advantage of some of their sales.

Now here's the thing with order quantity, and it's where my advice differs from a lot of other opinions out there: You don't have to buy 2,500 business cards just because VistaPrint tells you it's the cheapest.

Give yourself some freedom to change your mind about your design two months from now. Maybe you'll learn a new skill or become an apostille agent, wedding officiant, or something else amazing under the Notary umbrella. Our businesses are constantly evolving, and our business cards should evolve along with them.

Buy 100 to 250 cards at a time instead.

Sure, it's a few cents per unit more.

But being proud of handing out your business card is as important as having one in the first place. I can't tell you how many Notaries hand me a business card with phone numbers scratched out, name changes penciled in, or domain names written on the back. It looks unprofessional, and there's no need for that. Buy smaller batches and make any changes in reorders as you go.

Date Completed:

Challenge Review

Notes or initial observations:

What worked:

What didn't work:

What will you continue to do?

What will you do differently next time?

DAY 14
JOIN NOTARYREVIEWS.ORG

Are you looking for companies that will hire you as an independent contractor/Notary Public?

There are thousands of them out there!

The best resource I've found for aggregating these companies is Carrie Rivera and her Notary Reviews community. When you join this community, you'll get access to Carrie's list of over 1,000 hiring companies that includes contact information and other details about each company and its owners.

The most valuable part, though, is that these companies are often reviewed by your Notary peers, so you can learn which companies you'll most likely want to work for, and which you'll want to avoid.

Her list includes signing services, title/escrow companies, attorneys, and even industries that serve on the peripheral of loan signings, such as car loan companies, field inspection services, etc.

Today's challenge, assuming you're looking for more hiring companies, is to take one of these steps:

- Join Notary Reviews at the membership level that serves you best. You can visit NotaryReviews.org to do so, or find the direct link on the Readers Resource Website at www.NotaryCoach.com/90.

- If you are already a member of Notary Reviews, participate in the community by posting reviews of any companies you love to work with (or don't love to work with). You can find the direct link to where to post your ratings or reviews on the Readers Resource Website at www.NotaryCoach.com/90.

Remember that reviews are a way to give back and help those on the same journey, beside or behind you. Your contributions are truly important!

Date Completed:

Challenge Review

Notes or initial observations:

What worked:

What didn't work:

What will you continue to do?

What will you do differently next time?

DAY 15
IDENTIFY A NEW SPECIALTY
NOTARY WORK OPPORTUNITY

I think we can all agree that diversifying your services and revenue streams is critically important, right?

Today's challenge is about moving from random general Notary work (GNW) to specialization in your field.

My friend, Laura Biewer, is credited with coining the term "Specialty Notary Work" (SNW), to categorize those special niches within our industry that are deserving of more attention, training, and skill. In other words, specialization.

With the skill sets and mindsets that often accompany specialization comes more joy, more work, and more revenue.

Why?

Because with clarity comes customers.

Our Day 15 challenge is to identify a specialty that you either love working with OR make the most revenue in (or see some potential to do so).

Here are some ways to grease the wheels on that:

- Start with the obvious: loan signings (yup, that's a specialty too), estate planning documents, international adoptions, title transfers, retirement docs, etc.

- Then turn to old man Google. Search "most common notarized documents" or "documents you never expected to be notarized" or anything else you can think of, and see what jumps out at you.

- Take a trip down memory lane with your Journal of Notarial Acts. What are some of the documents you've encountered in the course of day-to-day business? Anything interesting? Research and find a market.

There are over one billion documents notarized each year in the U.S.

Opportunity is everywhere, and people need your services. Your job today is to find those people.

NBB Resource: *Laura Biewer is one of our founders of NBB and a core faculty member. She teaches a monthly live call on SNW. One of her lessons was a step-by-step framework on identifying a new specialty: "Laura Biewer Teaches Specialty Notary Work and How to Identify Specialty Niches." See where to find it using a short video on the Readers Resource Website at www.NotaryCoach.com/90.*

Challenge Review

Notes or initial observations:

What worked:

What didn't work:

What will you continue to do?

What will you do differently next time?

DAY 16
IDENTIFY YOUR IDEAL CUSTOMER

With clarity comes customers.

This is so important I'm going to say it again: *With clarity comes customers.*

When you know who your ideal customer is, everything you say and do can be aligned to attract them.

So, today's challenge is to get crystal clear about your ideal customer.

There are no wrong answers here! You get to choose your ideal customer (how cool is that?).

Even with no wrong answers, there is CLEAR and there is VAGUE. Remember today's theme—with clarity . . . **COMES CUSTOMERS!**

So below I've shared some questions and tips to prompt you, and you can run as fun, crazy, and specific as you want. Remember, we're not saying that we won't work with anyone but ideal clients (yet), but we are placing an order for exactly what we want in our dream business. And that's the power you hold with this business, and in life, really—you get to create it how you want it.

Now, if you have a brain like mine, you might appreciate a giant sticky note on the wall for this exercise. If not that, maybe use a notebook or something you can freestyle in. Or, if you're one of "those people," I suppose you can type it out too. :-)

How to identify your ideal customer:

There are two questions you can ask yourself to prime the pump:

1. Who do I LOVE to serve?

2. Where do I make the most money?

Even though I value the ideas that often come with these two questions, they're limited to our current or previous experience. So, we have to dive deeper.

Here are some other considerations for clarifying your ideal customer:

- Who actually needs my services the most? (Relates VERY closely to yesterday's challenge!)

- What do they really need or want from me? (Hint: It's probably NOT just a stamp.)

- Who is someone (position, person) you haven't yet worked with, but think you may want to?

- What are their goals, and how can you help them to reach them?

- What are some of their fears and challenges?

- How do you want to feel while you're working with them? (Huge lesson for me: Money isn't everything. If they pay you hordes of cash but treat you like crap, it's not worth it. Clarify the feelings surrounding your working relationship.)

Get as specific as possible.

Knowing who you WANT as a customer impacts your blog articles, social media posts, event attendance, networking, professional attire—everything!

You don't have to drift through this business taking scraps from the big kids' table.

Get clear. Get intentional. Get Busy.

As most of you know, I love this business and I'm still in the field as a Notary. My new focus has been estate planning appointments because I enjoy them, and with full presentation of documents (not just a stamp), they can be pretty lucrative. And . . . I am not interested in quibbling over $65 appointments anymore. So, I did this exercise for myself to help identify exactly who I want to work for at this stage in my career.

Here's what that looks like:

My ideal client is . . .

Family or estate attorneys (or their financial planning partners) who service decamillionaire clients (net worth over $10 million) and beyond with beautiful offices at or near the Biltmore Financial District in Phoenix, OR they're actively building their own virtual law firm, designing their own dream life. These clients prioritize their time and convenience, and appreciate prompt, friendly, and professional service with my casual, conversational style. Premium fees are set and agreed to from the onset of the partnership and I am included as part of the attorney value proposition to their clients. The staff and attorneys in these offices are also warm, friendly, and respectful, committed to a win-win for their clients and for their vendor partners like me. I look forward to getting their orders, knowing the exchange will be fun, mutually beneficial, and serving a valuable need. They have significant volume to support me, and do not hesitate to refer me to their colleagues at every opportunity. The documents are clean, accurate, and orderly, and the appointments run smoothly and efficiently. I meet interesting people at each and every appointment and are encouraged to stay in touch and cultivate longer relationships. Payment is prompt, usually within hours or days.

This has served me well so far, guys! I already have two new attorney clients who pay between $250 and $400 for fully presented estate-planning appointments. And I've also already determined several who will *not* be a good fit for me and my style.

Why?

Because of the paragraph above. I'm doing my research, finding out what my ideal clients are trying to build (especially with the virtual law firms), and using keywords in my communications that demonstrate my understanding and commitment to their cause and clients. I can paint the picture showing how I fit into their business and goals.

The clarity I've found has literally brought me more clients. This exercise can do the same for you.

Date Completed:

Challenge Review

Notes or initial observations:

What worked:

What didn't work:

What will you continue to do?

What will you do differently next time?

DAY 17
MAKE A LIST OF CONFERENCES OR TRAININGS THAT INTRIGUE YOU

Running a business as a solo-preneur is harder than most people admit.

I honor you for being here and taking massive action toward growing your business and meeting your goals.

Let's get to today's challenge!

Building new skills, staying up to date on industry standards, and continuously learning are extremely important to our success.

For today's challenge, identify at least five training events or conferences you'd like to attend in the next twelve months.

These events can be online OR in person and will serve two main purposes:

1. To learn from the content delivered at the event, as well as from any morsels from the universe that get dropped into your brain in those surroundings

2. To enhance your peer network. We need each other—for support, understanding, referrals, and friendship.

Keeping that in mind, it's time to tap into your current peer network and get some guidance, opinions, and counsel on what events might be right for you. I'll give you a few ideas below but remember, this is YOUR business. There are no rules.

Notary Training Events and Conferences for Your Consideration:

*   The Notary Symposium (Nov.)

*   The NNA Conference (June)

*   The Montana 406 Notary Conference (May)

*   Tuesday Notary Titans (Tuesdays)

*   Real World Notary Training for Your State with Laura Biewer (Varies)

- Google Business Profile Training for Notaries with Jim Allen

- Amazing trainers in your state

- Notary Business Builder (Varies)

- LSS Conference (Varies)

- The Philly Notary Social (Sept.)

Now it's your turn! Ask your network and do your own research on Aunt Google. There are events for every style and budget. Get intentional about your growth; otherwise you risk aimlessness and mediocrity.

Once you've identified five events that look good to you, start reserving your space. Either buy a ticket to the event if necessary, or add it to your calendar so you don't forget to attend.

And SHOW UP!

That's half the battle.

There are also ways you can optimize your experience and connections while at the events, but for now, let's just identify five events you want to attend and start making arrangements to do so.

NBB Resource: *Expanding your peer network is one of the thirteen opportunities I teach about in NBB for the full Top of Mind Method. I created a worksheet page you can download to keep track of your five events. Find it on the Readers Resource Website at www.NotaryCoach.com/90.*

Date Completed:

Challenge Review

Notes or initial observations:

What worked:

What didn't work:

What will you continue to do?

What will you do differently next time?

DAY 18
CREATE A REFERRAL LIST

Today's challenge is a fun exercise!

Being a resource to your network will help you stand out more than anything else. And here's the thing: Helping people get what they need or want is NOT limited to your capacity as a Notary Public.

You're an active citizen living in your city/state/country/world, and you've garnered some experience, wisdom, and favorite things through life.

In today's challenge, you get to organize all of your favorite people, places, and things and have them at the ready for when your network is ISO (in search of) something or someone to make their life better.

Today, you're going to create a referral list.

Here are some examples of what can go on your list of favorite things/referral list:

- Real estate agents
- Loan officers
- Handyman services
- Breakfast joint
- Coffeehouse
- Romantic restaurant
- Best sunset view location
- Meeting room
- Networking group
- You name it!

This is so important to your success that I teach it as part of the full Top of Mind Method in Notary Business Builder. I've created a worksheet to help prompt you. Feel free to download it from the Readers Resource Website at www.NotaryCoach.com/90 and use as you wish!

Once you have the start of your referral list, keep it front and center and update it regularly. You are always meeting new people, going to new places, and trying new things.

Then, LOOK for ways to use the list!

On social media, my network is constantly posting for referrals by writing "ISO best Thai restaurant in Phoenix," or "ISO honest mechanic," or "ISO real estate agent who specializes in Ahwatukee."

These opportunities to be a resource aren't only online either. They come up in conversations, appointments, while standing in line, and even while dining in restaurants.

I still get text messages from old friends for suggestions on breakfast burritos, specialists of this or that, or martinis. I've always "got a guy/gal for that."

Being a resource is just another way to keep yourself top of mind.

Now get to it!

Date Completed:

Challenge Review

Notes or initial observations:

What worked:

What didn't work:

What will you continue to do?

What will you do differently next time?

DAY 19
SEND A NOTE TO A NEW ACQUAINTANCE

It's time to put your note-writing kit to good use today.

Today's challenge is to send a warm note to someone you just met.

Whether you met them at an appointment, a networking event, or through a friend, they're a candidate for a note.

Here's what you do:

- Track down their address—the easiest way is to just ask them for it.

- Write out a quick note like, "Hey Samantha, it was such a pleasure to meet you the other day. I loved hearing about your travels through Peru. Cheers to new adventures, ahead! –Bill." If this is more of a professional connection, you can even sign as "Bill (the Notary)," and include your phone number.

- Avoid including business cards or branding of any kind. This is simply a nice note, from one human to another.

- Mail it.

Make a habit of doing this and you'll change your life.

Date Completed:

Challenge Review

Notes or initial observations:

What worked:

What didn't work:

What will you continue to do?

What will you do differently next time?

DAY 20
CONNECT WITH SOMEONE ON
A DIFFERENT PLATFORM

Let's enter the orbit of our ideal customers today.

Choose someone from your network whom you follow on social media, whether it be LinkedIn, Facebook, YouTube, Instagram, TikTok, Twitter, or another platform.

Pick someone who delivers content you personally find valuable OR pick one of your ideal clients you follow.

For today's challenge, find that person on a different platform where you're not currently connected and start following and engaging with them there.

For instance, you might subscribe to my Notary training YouTube channel here: https://www.youtube.com/notarycoach

And you can also find me on Instagram, where I share both business and personal threads: https://www.instagram.com/billsoroka/

And then, of course, I am pretty much all business (fun!) on LinkedIn here: https://www.linkedin.com/in/billsoroka/

Please feel free to connect with me on any or all of those platforms! But if you do . . . I don't count for today's challenge.

You have to find someone besides me to connect with on a different platform.

Make a habit of this and you'll give yourself more exposure to connection opportunities in your network.

Challenge Review

Notes or initial observations:

What worked:

What didn't work:

What will you continue to do?

What will you do differently next time?

DAY 21
RESPOND TO ALL REVIEWS

As a small business owner in your city, you probably already know the importance of acquiring reviews.

It's estimated that 97% of consumers make hiring/buying decisions based on reviews.

And, if you've garnered the courage to ask for reviews—and implemented a system for doing so—then maybe you have a few (or more) online already. One of my colleagues in Phoenix, Mike, has this dialed in well. As of this writing, he has over 300 customer reviews on Google!

Positive reviews lead to more business.

So today, your challenge is to respond to every single review you have (it's going to be a long day for Mike!).

Sometimes, reviews get taken for granted and we don't respond to each one. Let's look at this from another perspective. What if you were supporting a small bakery around the corner from your house. You love their blueberry muffins and cinnamon tea, so every weekend you try to stop by at least once to enjoy. One Saturday morning, the owner is there working the cash register and you let him know how much you enjoy his goods.

You: *"I just have to tell you that I love coming to your place each weekend. I think you bake the best blueberry muffins I've ever had. And thank you for brewing a delicious decaf tea. It's been so hard to find a place with tea that tastes good but doesn't get me all wired with caffeine."*

Him: <crickets> He just stands there staring at you, waiting for the next customer in line.

That's what it's like when a business owner doesn't respond to an online review. It's a totally missed opportunity for deeper connection!

Instead of crickets, take a few extra minutes to thoughtfully and warmly respond to each of your reviews.

Google makes responding to reviews very easy, and most other platforms allow you to respond as well.

At the very minimum, you can add a simple "Thank you!"

But I am going to encourage you to do more. "Thank you" is better than nothing, but we're in the middle of a 90-day challenge, so I don't think you're here to merely scrape by on bare minimums, right?

Let's use these reviews as a way to deepen our connection with a customer we've already served AND show prospective customers that we are committed to that level of deeper relationships.

Try responding something like this instead, in your own "voice":

Response from the owner: "Thank you so much, Julie! Being able to help kind customers like you and your family are exactly why I became a Notary Public in Pittsburgh. I know you have lots of options when choosing a mobile Notary, and I am honored that I was able to serve you. Please say hi to your mother, and give a kiss to Fido for me. Keep an eye on your snail mail, as I have a little something headed your way. I also recorded a short video response for you here: [Include YouTube video link]."

Next level, right?

Consider these suggestions when you respond:

- Be warm and heartfelt in your response. If possible, mention something directly relating to your interactions, appointment, and relationship.

- Gently include some of the keywords you hope to rank for in Google. Notice in the above example I use "Notary Public in Pittsburgh" and "mobile Notary." Do not stuff your response with keywords, though. Just be authentic and strategic, and let your words flow conversationally.

- If you haven't already sent a thank-you note, consider doing it now. Don't write, "I have a little something headed your way" if you don't actually have something headed their way. Sidenote: The "little something" is simply a thank-you card. You don't have to send any other gifts.

- And these thank-you videos are truly next level and will help you stand out WAY above the crowd. In each video, you can reiterate what you mentioned in the response, and maybe take it a little deeper. It's easy to upload them to YouTube, either publicly or unpublished, and then share the link.

And yes! You can go back to ALL your reviews, no matter how old they are. Start with the most recent and work your way back.

Now get to work on those responses!

Date Completed:

Challenge Review

Notes or initial observations:

What worked:

What didn't work:

What will you continue to do?

What will you do differently next time?

DAY 22
GET A CRM

Customer Relationship Management, or CRM, is software that helps you organize, track, and manage all your contact data and interactions so that you can more easily stay in touch with your clients and leads.

A CRM system provides a centralized place to compile all your contact information for current and past clients, prospects, and even friends and family.

Once you input your contacts, you can tag each with your own label so they're easy to find and group together as needed, such as when planning an email or postcard campaign or sending holiday cards.

There are also designated areas for notes so you can add highlights from your meetings, appointments, and conversations for ready reference as you cultivate your relationships.

A good CRM is worth its weight in gold, especially if you have plans to take your business into the atmospheric levels.

Today's challenge is to do a little research and find the right CRM for your own business.

When it comes to CRMs, I've tried a LOT of them! I'll share the names of a few that I've dabbled in, but I am also going to tell you I didn't enjoy working with any of them. I found them to be either too robust—with too many features for me as a solo-preneur—or too clunky—not ideal for road warriors like you and me. Still, I tried them, because I know CRM is an important tool. Ultimately, we partnered with Rapid Funnel and built our own, which I'll share farther below. You may find a different CRM works for you.

A few CRMs to explore:

- Monday.com
- Salesforce.com
- Hubspot.com

When it comes down to it, what you're really looking for in a CRM is to be able to do the following:

- Easily use it on the fly and in your car after an appointment

- Label contacts and leave notes

- Easily assign automated email campaigns

- Broadcast emails to all or sectors of your network

- Schedule reminders of important dates or to follow up

As mentioned above, we created a system with the TOMM app, powered by Rapid Funnel, with these very features (and so much more). I put together a few demos that you can watch here: https://www.notarycoach.com/tomm.

TOMM is available only to members of Notary Business Builder. And, you're totally invited to join us in NBB, of course! We have a great deal for you simply for participating in this challenge.

Click the link on the Readers Resource Website for NBB Special Pricing or go to www.notarycoach.com/nbbfresh.

As I teach in the Top of Mind Method, we have at least thirteen opportunities to make a great first impression, fortify our value, and deepen our relationships as people work their way through our business—our Notary Funnel. Having a CRM simplifies and even automates some of that process for you.

Date Completed:

Challenge Review

Notes or initial observations:

What worked:

What didn't work:

What will you continue to do?

What will you do differently next time?

DAY 23
CREATE A SYSTEM FOR OBTAINING REVIEWS

Earlier in the NFC, I mentioned the importance of reviews and encouraged you to respond to each and every one you receive. If you're like most of the students I coach across the country, that activity probably got you thinking a little bit about your process for asking clients for reviews.

Most Notaries I talk to know reviews are important, and they know they should be asking for them, but . . . they're not being consistent.

And that's all it is!

Inconsistent activity gets inconsistent results.

No need for shame and judgment.

Let's just get consistent!

Today's challenge is to create a script and a process for asking each qualified client for an honest review—and then make it a habit.

I specified "qualified client" because there will clearly be some clients you won't want to ask for a review. Sometimes they're "Grumpy Gus" or "Cranky Connie." Sometimes we make mistakes or rub people the wrong way (and vice versa). Don't worry about those clients. Focus on the majority of your appointments with awesome clients you get along with who will want to support your business.

Here's how to establish your habit:

1. When do you want to ask? You can decide if you want to ask immediately after the appointment, the next day, or a week later. It's totally up to you!

2. How do you want to ask? You can decide if you will ask face to face at the appointment, or later in a text message or email.

3. What will you say? You can choose verbiage that matches your personality and brand.

4. What's the call to action (CTA)? You can decide where to suggest the client leaves their review (Google, Yelp, LinkedIn, etc.).

Here's what your answers to the above might look like:

1. I want to ask within a couple hours of the appointment.

2. I prefer to send a quick text message with a thank-you and my request.

3. I'll say, "It was so nice meeting you! I wonder if you could do me a favor. Reviews help my small business thrive. If I sent you the link to do so, would you be willing to leave me an honest review of my services today?"

4. I want the review to appear on my Google Business Profile, so I'll send them a direct link to the review section of my profile.

When you start to consistently *ask* for reviews, you'll start to consistently *get* reviews.

Date Completed:

Challenge Review

Notes or initial observations:

What worked:

What didn't work:

What will you continue to do?

What will you do differently next time?

DAY 24
TAKE THE VIA INSTITUTE'S
CHARACTER ASSESSMENT

I've always enjoyed learning.

Today I'll introduce you to a tool I use to get intentional about my learning.

Your challenge is to take the free Survey of Character Strengths offered by the VIA Institute, described as follows:

"The VIA Survey of Character Strengths is a free self-assessment that takes less than 15 minutes and provides a wealth of information to help you understand your best qualities. VIA Reports provide personalized, in-depth analysis of your free results, including actionable tips to apply your strengths to find greater well-being."

I take this survey once a year, usually in December or January. I do this for two main reasons:

- I think it's important and interesting to track my growth and pay attention to how I am showing up in the world. This has proven helpful in a "people business."

- My survey results help me get intentional with my reading and learning for personal development in the year ahead.

This survey ranks and categorizes the 24 character strengths positive psychology has identified in all of us. Based on my personalized results, I decide what I want to work on for the coming year. Then I find books, classes, and workshops that are topical for that strength. For example, one quarter, I chose curiosity as the strength to work on. In another quarter, I chose gratitude. In yet another, it was forgiveness.

These are the characteristics that round out our human nature. It's how we begin to take responsibility for our emotional wake—how we make people feel when we leave the room or walk away from a conversation.

I call this your likeability factor. It's the most influential pillar of the four that make for solid relationships.

Yes, the first three are important too—competence, confidence, and integrity—but without likeability, our business becomes harder than it needs to be.

Use the Survey of Character Strengths to identify where you're at right now. Then choose something about yourself to learn more about.

Keep going.

Take the Survey of Character Strengths on the Readers Resource Website at www.NotaryCoach.com/90.

It's totally free to take the survey!

Just know your results will vary over the years.

From their website (www.viacharacter.org):

Why Do Character Strengths Matter?

Character strengths are the positive parts of your personality that make you feel authentic and engaged. You possess all 24 character strengths in different degrees, giving you a unique character strengths profile. Research shows that understanding and applying your strengths can help

- Boost confidence
- Increase happiness
- Strengthen relationships
- Manage problems
- Reduce stress
- Accomplish goals
- Build meaning and purpose
- Improve work performance

Discover your greatest qualities and begin using your strengths to build your best life.

Challenge Review

Notes or initial observations:

What worked:

What didn't work:

What will you continue to do?

What will you do differently next time?

DAY 25
MAKE IT EASY TO BOOK

I recently heard an interesting statistic. It suggested that 70% of consumers (your customers) would prefer to book or buy online than pick up the phone and have to call someone.

For you and me, as consumers ourselves, this probably makes sense, right? I do everything online, from ordering dinner through an app to ordering empty boxes to help me move.

For your business, though, have you made that switch to help your own prospective clients book your services online?

Apparently, it's what they want.

Today's challenge is to automate your booking calendar.

I know it can be scary.

There's the whole technology piece, and I know that can be intimidating.

Then there's the fear that people will be booking appointments all willy-nilly, all day and all night.

Totally legit fears, for sure.

Rest assured, there are some user-friendly services that make automated booking a breeze. I'll share a couple with you down below.

And the really cool thing is that you still maintain control over your schedule. This is YOUR business. The scheduling services below allow you to set the rules for when you want to accept appointments, how much time you want in between appointments, how to label and set up different types of appointments—you name it. You can even integrate payment methods if you want!

I get to talk to LOTS of Notaries across the country, and those who are killin' it with specialty and general Notary work are automating their booking calendars. It's worth a serious look for you.

Here are two services to research and explore:

- Calendly: http://www.calendly.com/

- Acuity Scheduling: http://www.acuityscheduling.com/

I use Calendly for my automated booking. I created a quick ten-minute walk-through if you want to see how easy it is to use. Watch it on the Readers Resource Website at www.NotaryCoach.com/90.

Date Completed:

Challenge Review

Notes or initial observations:

What worked:

What didn't work:

What will you continue to do?

What will you do differently next time?

DAY 26
TAKE TEN BREATHS BEFORE

One of the ways I maintain peace of mind on hectic days and stressful situations is a breathing exercise I'd like to share with you for Day 26 of our challenge.

As a hustling solo-preneur, we run into all kinds of stressful situations in our day:

- Traffic delays

- Weird documents

- Expired ID

- New clients

- Attorneys and/or real estate agents in our appointments

- Cranky people

- Walking into stranger's homes

- Strange homes!

- Oh yeah, and then our normal lives, too

Using the simple deep-breathing exercise below has been proven to decrease stress, lower blood pressure, and increase overall well-being. All while improving vitality and mood.

Today's challenge is to take ten deep breaths. And then remind yourself to do it again every time you feel stressed, angry, sad, or even just plain tired.

Don't want to do ten? You rebel, you. That's okay. Take three deep breaths. It still helps. Scale to your needs.

When I first started this exercise after learning it from a mentor, I did what I tend to do with these things—I over-thought it. I was running around holding my breath, evaluating average breathing cycles of the human population, obsessing over whether I was taking a deep enough breath . . .

It doesn't have to be like that.

My coach, Linda, introduced me to a quick and easy way to breathe and I blended these two strategies.

Use a four-count.

1, 2, 3, 4 as you breathe in through your nose at a nice, slow pace.

1, 2, 3, 4 as you breathe out through your mouth at a nice, slow pace.

I like to do this in the car right before an appointment and again as I am walking up to the door. It helps to center me, calm the nerves, and bring me to the ultimate place of service and connection.

Date Completed:

Challenge Review

Notes or initial observations:

What worked:

What didn't work:

What will you continue to do?

What will you do differently next time?

DAY 27
START A BLOG

Ready to keep expanding your comfort zone?

Today's challenge is to start a blog (or if you already have a blog, write a new post).

I already know that most Notaries in the country do not have a blog yet, so this is likely a new opportunity for you.

A blog is simply an online place where you can write your thoughts, share information, and provide additional value to your clients and prospective customers.

So why does having a blog matter for a mobile Notary and loan signing agent?

Here are a few good reasons to have a blog IF you plan on being the go-to Notary in your city:

- Every piece of fresh content you create and post is an opportunity to demonstrate your wisdom, knowledge, skill, and expertise.

- Structured with intentional and balanced keywords, posting fresh blog content regularly is likely to bolster your website's SEO.

- Blogs can help you attract your ideal customers, instead of default customers.

- Original content can lead to connection and speaking opportunities as well as introductions to industry professionals.

- Your blog can help solve people's problems by answering common questions or serving up info on current events.

- Blogs that showcase your personality allow your prospective customers to get to know your values and style.

People work with who they know, like, and trust. With every piece of thoughtful content, packed full of value you provide, you give people the chance to get to know, like, and trust YOU.

Blogging is free, and it ranks right up there with Google Business Profile as low-hanging fruit that credentialed professionals like you and me can use to help customers find us when they need us.

Here are some common blogging platforms:

- Yup, Google Business Profile can be used as a blog with their "Posts" feature and more.

- LinkedIn allows you to write and share articles.

- Almost every website builder or template service, such as WordPress, Wix, GoDaddy, etc., has a blog feature.

- There are no rules, and there are LOTS of independent blogging profiles you can link to your website.

Blog when you want, but be intentional and consistent when you do. Choose to post monthly, quarterly, weekly, or daily, and then keep at it. Do not create a blog without a plan to keep it reasonably updated. A blog with only a few stale posts from three years ago may indicate a lack of follow-through on your part or can even leave the impression you're not up to speed on the latest topics in the field.

Better not to create a blog at all than to post to it only sporadically. But do bear in mind the posts don't need to be lengthy, just informative, so it's not as daunting as it might appear.

Know who your audience is! Remember the work we did earlier in this challenge on identifying your ideal customer? Keep this in mind when you choose topics to write about. What do those customers want or need to learn?

A good practice is to make a list of topics in advance so you'll have a rough schedule to work from. You can even create outlines for some of your future posts to make the task of writing that much easier. You can find a list of 52 topics on the Reader's Resource Website at www.NotaryCoach.com/90.

The challenge today is to simply start a blog. You don't have to write anything today; just get it set up. Write your first post tomorrow.

Okay, now get to it!

NBB Resource: *Check out the incredible course we put together to help NBB members create a blog, or even a vlog (video blog), and the system you can use to distribute your content through email and social media. Inside NBB you will find access to the "Get Known Strategy" course.*

Challenge Review

Notes or initial observations:

What worked:

What didn't work:

What will you continue to do?

What will you do differently next time?

DAY 28
RESEARCH A TARGET FROM YOUR
FAB 100 LIST ON SOCIAL

Today we're going to use one of the resources from earlier in the challenge—your Fab 100 list. Remember, that's the list of people or companies that you might want to work with.

This list could include escrow officers, real estate agents, loan officers, attorneys, hospitals, care centers, school systems—you name it.

Your Day 28 Challenge is to research one name from your Fab 100 List.

And if you want to get all extra about it, you can research even more than one. Depending on what projects I have going on, I may do five or ten of these each day to help me prepare for connection and outreach later.

But if you're not used to this yet, start with one. Choose just one name from your list, and let's do some research.

First, here are some tools for research in today's world:

- Google
- Facebook
- LinkedIn
- Public library resources
- Business journal and similar publications

What to look for in research:

- Office locations
- Names of those who work in the office
- Social platforms
- Civic activities/philanthropy
- Current projects or niche focus

- Challenges or opportunities

- Leadership names, history, experience

- Big wins or "In the News" items

Then, use the "2 in 5" strategy.

Whether on their website, their social media pages, or even right from your Fab 100 spreadsheet, look for **two things in five minutes** that stand out to you. You're looking for super low-hanging fruit here.

Find things that

- You can easily relate to

- You can talk about on a deeper level

- Inspire you to want to work with this person or company

- Or, even signal that this company or person is *not* one you want to work with

Document your findings in your Fab 100 spreadsheet or file so you can use them as a reference as you start reaching out to build relationships. The most successful mobile Notaries and loan signing agents are able to kick off conversations that have a foundation in something deeper than sales. They find something other than themselves to talk about.

That's what today is all about—flipping the conversation to be about your prospect and their dreams, not yours.

Consider making this challenge part of your own Daily Do's and you'll always have someone to talk to about business—both theirs and yours.

Date Completed:

Challenge Review

Notes or initial observations:

What worked:

What didn't work:

What will you continue to do?

What will you do differently next time?

DAY 29
MAKE YOUR REFERRAL LIST BEAUTIFUL

Feel like getting creative today?

Today's challenge is to beautify your referral list.

Remember that from a previous challenge way back on Day 18? If you didn't do it then, that's okay; you can do it today as well.

Your referral list is important because it keeps your network of trusted brands, people, and services top of mind for you so they're easy to refer to others that need them. THIS is a great way for you to bring value to your overall network and make you memorable.

The most effective way to make referrals, of course, is one-on-one connection with introductions.

And another way to effectively use your referral list is to beautify it, brand it, and make it easy to send out or post.

Here's the workflow for this:

- I've found the easiest way to create beautiful graphics, with zero design skills, is Canva: https://www.canva.com/. Canva has both a paid and a free version. I've found the paid version at $13 a month or so to be worth every penny.

- You can choose a template from the Infographic or Poster section (or any template that calls to you).

- Organize your referral list into a theme, e.g., real estate contacts, medical team contacts, productivity hacks, personal development books, etc.

- Pick your top five or so from each category.

- Create a graphic that includes your favorite person's name, company, and contact info. Make sure they know to mention your name when they reach out!

- Don't forget to include your own personal branding and contact information as well.

- Download your graphic as both a PDF and a PNG (may need the premium edition for this).

- NBB members can create a TOMM Resource that can easily be sent out and tracked when opened. See the Resource Workshops replay in the archive.

- Use the PNG graphic to spotlight your favorite people with the occasional social media post. This gives you something to talk about on social, provides valuable content to your network, and supports the very people you love to work with.

I created a quick video on how to beautify your referral list using Canva. Watch it on the Readers Resource Website at www.NotaryCoach.com/90.

Challenge Review

Notes or initial observations:

What worked:

What didn't work:

What will you continue to do?

What will you do differently next time?

DAY 30
RESEARCH AND REGISTER FOR
A CLIENT-GETTING EVENT

Your challenge today is the first step of a networking trick used by super connectors and high performers in many industries.

The plan is fairly simple: Attend five client-getting events each year.

The key, though, is to be intentional and strategize your plan in advance to ensure you attend the events that will be of most value to you.

So, what's a client-getting event? Pretty much any semi-structured learning or networking event where your ideal customers congregate.

Let's start there. You'll remember earlier in the challenge we did some work to help you identify who your ideal customers might be. Hopefully you came up with a pretty good idea of who brings you joy or revenue (or both) in your day-to-day work.

Well, guess what? Nearly anyone you choose as an ideal customer will likely belong to some sort of industry association or regulatory body that holds meetings, conferences, training sessions, cocktail parties, charity events, or other activities that bring their like-minded colleagues and associates together.

And one way or another, they hold a space for you, too, as a member, a vendor, a sponsor, or a friend.

Today's challenge is to identify five client-getting events you can attend in the next twelve months. And, if you really want to be all extra about it, reserve your seat at one of them today.

Let's look at a couple of examples:

- If you chose attorneys as your ideal customers, you might explore your state or local bar association membership options and events. Keep in mind there are niches and specialties within the legal profession. Look for legal organizations that support your niche, like estate planning, etc.

- If you chose senior living situations, you might explore associations that support the admin staff, nurses, or even the seniors themselves.

- If you chose escrow officers, you might consider events or membership at the American Land Title Association or the various mortgage lenders associations.

There are lots of ways to participate in groups and associations like these. Get curious and explore. Can you attend as a guest? Are there membership options for peripheral industry personnel? What about vendor registration or sponsorship?

The options are endless and you deserve a seat at the table.

Let's be real here. If you truly believe you bring the passion and expertise to the table that will best serve your customers, then by not showing up where they are, you're doing them a huge disservice.

In addition to checking industry and association websites, you can also find relevant events listings on Facebook, LinkedIn, and Meetup.com.

I can't wait to hear what you find and what events you'll attend.

And remember, online events count. In-person counts. Free counts. Paid counts.

Connect. Connect. Connect.

Client-getting events are different from peer networking events. Both are equally important, but different. Peer events tend to be a little more comfortable for us because we relate so well, and we tend to like one another. Plus, Notaries can party! But your biggest growth will come from pushing the boundaries of your comfort zone by surrounding yourself with the very people you'd like to be of service to. I believe we're all simply one connection away from our dream client.

You just never know who you'll meet.

Date Completed:

Challenge Review

Notes or initial observations:

What worked:

What didn't work:

What will you continue to do?

What will you do differently next time?

DAY 31
PUT UP A WEBSITE

I still get this question all the time: Do I need a website?

I know everyone loves a black-and-white, all-encompassing answer, but the truth is, it just depends. It depends mainly on what it is you're trying to build here. And, since you're part of this Notary Funnel Challenge, and it seems to me that your goal is to grow your business, then I am going to say yeah, you probably need a website.

- Yes, Google Business Profile is important. And, yes, it has Pages, and a Post feature, and a place to list Services. It's actually pretty awesome and important.

- And, yes, social media platforms like Facebook, Instagram, and LinkedIn are important too. They give you access to lots of fresh new customers and millions of potential followers.

But here's the rub: Customers on someone else's platform, such as Google and Facebook, aren't really your customers. They belong to Google and Facebook.

You can have a billion followers on Facebook, but if you don't do something to connect *off* Facebook, then you're vulnerable to FB's rules, mandates, and algorithms. They could change one thing tomorrow that makes you lose contact with your audience.

Similarly, Google could abruptly throw you in what is commonly called "Google Jail" and suspend your account for no apparent reason, citing Terms of Service violations.

If all you have are other people's platforms, you're at risk.

Want to own your customers?

Step one is to have a website.

So your challenge today is to get a website.

I know, it's easier said than done.

I'll give you a few resources later, and right now I'm going to offer you some guidelines for constructing your site.

Here's what to include on your website:

- A homepage that immediately addresses and solves the problem of your ideal customers

- Keywords that your ideal customers are searching for on Google

- Easy and clickable contact information "above the fold" and on every page. Don't make them work to contact you!

- A separate page for each of your individual services, such as Apostille Agent, Estate Planning, Loan Signings, Fingerprinting, Wedding Officiant, etc.

- A way to automatically book appointments with you

- A blog feature so you can create content when you're ready

- A "Subscribe Now" field so you can capture emails. You don't have to have a plan yet for a newsletter or another way to use those emails, but collecting email addresses is how you build a business that lasts.

You can build your own website with tools such as these:

- Wix

- GoDaddy

- WordPress

Or, you can hire a website designer from a platform like these:

- Fiverr

- Upwork

If you choose to hire someone to help you, have them keep the design basic, and always be sure you have access to the "back end" of the site to make updates and changes later. You never want to be held hostage by someone else's schedule or ego.

For my website, I partnered with Green Monkey Marketing, led by my friend and NBB faculty member Tyler Botsford.

He's created several Notary website templates and offers the "in-between" or hybrid between do-it-yourself and done-for-you websites. You can purchase the website package and submit your changes to his team and they'll handle everything for you.

Then, on top of that, they offer video training on how to access the back end and learn to make all the changes and updates yourself!

You can explore the Notary Website Templates on the Readers Resource Website at www.NotaryCoach.com/90, or simply visit Tyler Botsford's site at https://greenmonkeymarketing.com/notary-website/.

Date Completed:

Challenge Review

Notes or initial observations:

What worked:

What didn't work:

What will you continue to do?

What will you do differently next time?

DAY 32
ADD A BANNER IMAGE TO LINKEDIN

You may very well have already created your LinkedIn profile as part of this Notary Funnel Challenge.

Or, maybe you created your LinkedIn profile after reading the book *Supercharge Your Notary Business with LinkedIn*, written by Sandra Long and me. (Find it on Amazon or at www.Notarycoach.com/books.)

And maybe you are just advanced enough to have already created your LinkedIn profile on your own. Kudos to you!

Today, we're going to take it up a notch.

Your Day 32 Challenge is to add a custom banner image to your LinkedIn profile.

As mentioned previously, my favorite way to create images these days is with Canva. Again, they offer both free and premium plans, so pick what is right for you.

Canva has a template series for LinkedIn banners, so the correct dimensions are all set in place and you can customize the design as you see fit.

Your banner image can highlight your services, values, and personality.

Have fun with this, and consider updating your banner every month or so. It helps keep your content fresh and relevant to your LinkedIn audience.

Plus, Notary professionals are always learning new skills and specialties, so you likely will be able to periodically switch up what you feature.

NBB Resource: *Members of NBB have access to LinkedIn consultant and trainer Sandra Long's exclusive course "LinkedIn Professional Profile." As part of the course, Sandra explains the intricacies of a popular banner image, and even provides templates you can use in the Notary world.*

Date Completed:

Challenge Review

Notes or initial observations:

What worked:

What didn't work:

What will you continue to do?

What will you do differently next time?

DAY 33
IDENTIFY THE BEST KEYWORDS TO USE TO BE FOUND

Ready to geek out on keywords?

It's okay if you roll your eyes, or run away.

Keywords are weird, confusing sometimes, and . . . important.

To break it down, keywords are words or phrases that your ideal customers are using when they search online using Google and other search engines for the products or services they need.

Your challenge today is to identify those keywords your ideal customers are using to find your services online.

Some of these may be obvious, like "Notary Near Me." Lots of people search for that.

But did you know many people search for "Notary Republics" too?

And "Public Notary"?

Even "jail notary" has traction in some markets.

But chances are you offer other services too. Here are additional words and phrases potential customers use to find our services:

- "Fingerprinting for teachers"

- "Wedding officiant for gay couples"

- "Insurance field inspections"

- "Express apostille services"

There are a few easy ways to identify the most effective keywords.

First, think like a customer. What will they need or want?

Second, think like a customer who doesn't really know what they need or want.

And third, use tools such as Keywords Everywhere, the Google Ads Keyword Tracker, and Rank Checker. Or, simply use Google Searches.

A bonus fourth tip is to consider adding your geographic location to whatever keywords you come up with, e.g., "Notary Phoenix," "Apostille Anaheim," "Fingerprinting in Duluth," etc.

Once you know what your potential customers are searching for, you can start solving their problems with your content.

Use your keywords and phrases in all your online content:

- Website

- Blog posts

- Videos

- Social media posts

- Electronic newsletters

- Text/email responses

The more you responsibly use keywords and provide value to the audience seeking this information, the more relevant you'll be in the eyes of Google Search. That means they will more likely pair you and your services with people who are searching for them.

Make a list of the best keywords you find and integrate them into your content. Revisit your keyword search regularly so you can continually keep your content updated.

Date Completed:

Challenge Review

Notes or initial observations:

What worked:

What didn't work:

What will you continue to do?

What will you do differently next time?

DAY 34
JOIN AN ONLINE GROUP
OF IDEAL CUSTOMERS

So, a few days ago, we talked about client acquisition events.

Attending five of those a year will change your life and your business.

And, did you know that in addition to events, there are very likely online groups packed full of your ideal customers?

Yep.

Believe it or not, we're all kind of in the same boat.

Whether we're solo-preneurs, directors, supervisors, managers, or employees, we're all trying to be of service and/or solve problems.

And there are entire industries built to help every single one of us succeed.

And within those industries are Groups!

- Facebook groups

- Circle groups

- Voxer groups

- Mighty Network groups

Your challenge today is to join a group that is FULL of your dream or ideal customers. (Do you see yet how important your ideal customer definitions can be?)

Once you're in, don't stress. No pressure. Simply observe, to begin. Note that some groups will ask that new members introduce themselves upon joining. In that case, just say hello and that you're glad to be there and look forward to being a part of the group. This may prompt some members to welcome you, providing an easy way to start connecting with people.

Later, once you've got the lay of the land, you can begin participating by joining in on discussions and sharing information, as appropriate, being careful to add value to the conversation. From there you can act on opportunities and introductions as they arise. Check Google, Facebook, and LinkedIn to find the right groups for you.

Date Completed:

Challenge Review

Notes or initial observations:

What worked:

What didn't work:

What will you continue to do?

What will you do differently next time?

DAY 35
REQUEST FEEDBACK FROM FRIENDS

All right, today we go deep into self-discovery and personal development.

The challenge with self-discovery is that we're often blinded by our own biases, emotions, and memories. We think we are different than how we are actually perceived by others. Part of growth is taking responsibility for how we show up to the world and other people, as well as the "emotional wake" we leave behind after an interaction.

To help you better understand that outside perception, there is a technique I've adapted from several mentors.

Your challenge today is to send an email requesting feedback from your top ten most trusted friends, family, colleagues, or advisors.

Here's how it works:

Send a carefully crafted email to ten people in your network whose opinion you trust and respect. Choose people who have seen you at your greatest, and perhaps even at your worst (for they have seen you rise).

The objective is to get some raw feedback on your strengths, weaknesses, and with any luck, maybe some of your blind spots. The nature of a blind spot is, of course, that you cannot see it. You do not know it exists, but there have likely been clues. You are a perceptive being and there is always some part of you that picks up on cues from others, whether it be in body language, word choices, or simply the fact that people no longer invite you to parties and lunches, ask you for advice, or share secrets with you, etc.

BEFORE you send an email requesting feedback, I highly recommend a quick conversation to gauge interest, either via phone, email, or text. Something like, "I am doing some personal development work and I'd love your perspective. Do you have a few minutes to respond to an email with some feedback?"

Then send an email similar to the one below. Feel free to adapt and edit to match your personality and relationship to the recipient.

"Hi _____,

Thank you so much for your willingness to help me out on this personal project. I truly appreciate your valuable time and your willingness to take this seriously.

I've chosen only a few of the most influential people in my life to assist with this—those who have challenged my way of thinking and who have helped raise my standards. I'm asking you because I trust and respect you, plus I can count on you for direct and honest responses.

As part of my project and inner work, I'd like to better understand how I "show up" to others.

From the outside looking in, I'd like to hear how you perceive some of my strengths—those things you think I am really good at.

And, I'd also like to hear about some of the weaknesses, or challenges, you might see me encountering regularly. Maybe I am not fully aware of them yet.

This is not a fishing expedition for compliments and ego boosts. I am on a quest to learn how I can best serve others, and your insight will help me grow and be better.

I appreciate any feedback you can provide on the following:

- *What characteristics, positive or negative, describe me?*

- *What talents and abilities have you noticed about me?*

- *From your perspective, how do people feel when they're around me?*

- *How do I do things in general? Do I consistently meet deadlines and deliver quality service or goods, or can I improve on that? Would you say I am a perfectionist or more of a "done-is-better-than-perfect" kind of person?*

- *What can you count on me for?*

And please share anything else you see as a core attribute of who I am and how I show up to our relationship.

I would be grateful if you could respond to this email within seven days if you are willing and able to help me. Please don't be shy about the feedback you provide. It will help me know what I need to know in order to grow.

Thank you for your support! I look forward to hearing back from you."

Once you send it, give people four or five days to respond. Even after you have primed them with a pre-request text, email, or phone call, and then have sent the carefully crafted email, some people will not respond right away. On day five or six, if you still haven't heard anything, you can send a gentle reminder that says something like this:

"Hi _____!

Just checking back regarding the request for feedback I sent you on [DATE].

If you'd still like to participate, I'd welcome a response anytime in the next few days. If you're running late, don't sweat it!

And if you've changed your mind, no worries. Just let me know—judgment-free zone here!

Thank you so much for being a part of my growth (again)!"

You'll likely get four to six responses. Don't take it personally if people don't respond at all. That has more to do with them than you. They're likely too busy, or too uncomfortable with uncomfortable conversations.

To help your respondents be more comfortable, you can set up a Google Form, and even a survey-style questionnaire, that allows for anonymity.

There's also no rule that says you have to stop at ten people. You're the boss. Send it to twenty people, or one hundred if you want, until you have some data to move on.

Don't be afraid of the responses.

I know this puts you in a vulnerable place.

Most of the responses will actually boost you up. You'll hear how kind you are. Or how you make people laugh. Or how intense and smart you are. Maybe you inspire others. Or turn heads when you walk in a room. Perhaps you listen well so others feel heard around you. Maybe you make people feel as though they are the only person on the planet when you talk to them.

All incredibly powerful gifts.

What, then, about potential weaknesses and blind spots?

Sure, some of these can feel like they come from left field. But usually not. Remember, you are a perceptive being. You know most of this stuff about yourself already. You may be lying to yourself. You may be stuffing it down somewhere. You might even be justifying it ("I can be mean because if I am always nice, people take advantage of me").

If you get some random, one-off type of feedback, take it with a grain of salt. If you hear it more than once, it's likely worth some attention.

This exercise serves two purposes:

- It shines the light on our blind spots.

- And it helps us celebrate our magnificence.

How cool is that?

Date Completed:

Challenge Review

Notes or initial observations:

What worked:

What didn't work:

What will you continue to do?

What will you do differently next time?

DAY 36
BECOME ORDAINED

Dearly beloved,

We are gathered here today, under this expansive "Notary Umbrella," to celebrate the union of services we have available as Notary Public.

Our topic today: Wedding Officiant, Celebrant, Ordained Minister, Wedding Solemnizer, Uniter of Love. Or, if you're a fan of *The Princess Bride*, what we're saying is, "Mawwidge is whut bwings us togevveh today."

I know that being a wedding officiant isn't for everyone, so no shame if this is just of no interest to you. Own your decision. But . . .

If there is a part of you that is intrigued about playing a part in the special celebration of the union between two people, read on.

Today's challenge is to become a Wedding Officiant in your state.

Here's what's interesting: You DO NOT need to be a Notary Public to be a wedding officiant.

Sure, a few states include wedding solemnization in their notarial acts, but you don't need that to perform wedding ceremonies.

In most states, nearly anyone is eligible to become an ordained minister to perform weddings.

It doesn't matter if you have a Notary commission or not.

So, if this is even remotely on your radar, let's get ordained today.

One of the best resources I've found for this is the Universal Life Church. They make it easy and inexpensive to become ordained to meet most state requirements for officiating weddings.

Find U.S. state wedding laws here: https://www.ulc.org/wedding-laws.

Why do this?

We're looking for joy, purpose, and revenue, right?

Adding wedding officiant services to your portfolio can tie right into that.

Today, by taking action, at the very minimum you leave yourself open to a new stream of joy and income.

Is that not worth the effort?

If you're like me, you may be open, even excited, about being a part of these special days for couples. And . . . you may also be terrified about how to actually do the job as a wedding officiant and provide a world-class experience that will button up the day and be remembered. For that reason, I found one of the top trainers in the world to coach me, Mark Allan Groleau, and looked to his Unboring!Wedding Officiant Academy to give me the framework I was craving.

If you want to be a wedding officiant who can provide more than the minimum, or more than the basic traditional wedding experience, then you will want to learn from Mark.

Check out his special pricing for Notaries for both of his programs at the link below or on the Readers Resource Website at www.NotaryCoach.com/90.

Learn all about how to become an Unboring!Wedding Officiant by visiting https://www.unboringweddingacademy.com/notarycoach.

Date Completed:

Challenge Review

Notes or initial observations:

What worked:

What didn't work:

What will you continue to do?

What will you do differently next time?

DAY 37
GET LISTED IN ALL RELEVANT
NOTARY DIRECTORIES

There are some solid online Notary directories that can help enhance your business and keep your phones ringing and dinging when you optimize your profiles.

Your challenge today is to make sure you are listed on as many free Notary directory websites as possible.

Most of them offer a free profile listing option, as well as a "premium" listing with enhanced features and visibility. Start with the free, or basic, profile listing and then you can upgrade as your budget allows. The following directories tend to have an excellent reputation for generating phone calls, so you should be able to recapture your investment in a premium listing at the very least.

Here are some directories to explore:

- www.NotaryCafe.com

- www.123Notary.com

- www.ReverseNotary.com (for Certified Reverse Mortgage Signing Professionals [CRMSP])

- www.SigningAgent.com (for Loan Signing Agents [LSA])

- www.NotaryRotary.com

- www.NotaryStars.com

These directories have either filled a niche or have recognition by search engines as an "authority" site in the industry. That means your optimized profile on these directories may rank higher when potential customers search for a "Notary Near Me."

Try not to overthink this too much. Done is better than perfect when it comes to your directory listings, and these will greatly enhance your digital presence.

NBB Resource: *Start with your LinkedIn Profile—Your "master profile." You have access to the complete LinkedIn Professional Profile Course to walk you through profile setup. And then you can easily copy and paste content from LinkedIn to these other directory profiles.*

Sandra Long, Ronnie Mickle, and I led a training session on exactly how to use LinkedIn as your "master profile." You can watch it on the Readers Resource Website at www.NotaryCoach.com/90.

Date Completed:

Challenge Review

Notes or initial observations:

What worked:

What didn't work:

What will you continue to do?

What will you do differently next time?

DAY 38
CREATE AN INTAKE FORM

By implementing the tool in today's challenge, I took a lot of the stress out of general and specialty Notary work (GNW/SNW) calls.

Before I created a basic intake form, or my "call record," as it was named at one time, these GNW/SNW calls always seemed to sideswipe me.

There would be unique locations, with unusual situations and sometimes bizarre ID or family history stories, that left me scrambling for the right questions.

I was thrown off my game, and certainly wasn't "Ready for Yes." In fact, there was a small part of me that was hoping for "No."

That's no way to run a business.

So I had a little conversation with myself, decided to fully embrace general Notary work (and the specialties within it), did some research, and built a call record. I saw other Notaries creating similar forms, my favorite name for which I learned from Kim Flanagan and Laura Biewer: Client Intake Form.

Your challenge today is to create or acquire a Client Intake Form for general and specialty Notary work.

If you already take lots of GNW/SNW calls, you may already have a flow. Consider writing it down.

If you don't have experience with GNW/SNW call flow yet, luckily Kim Flanagan has created a beautiful Client Intake Form she makes available for sale at Notary Allies. I'll include links below.

A good Client Intake Form will prompt you to ask questions that help you avoid surprises and set proper expectations for the customer.

You'll be reminded to ask about the entry requirements at the appointment location, witnesses, document requirements, and legal IDs. And so much more.

No one likes to waste their time or money. Not you. Not your customer.

A Client Intake Form can help minimize all that.

Enjoy today and be Ready for Yes the next time your phone rings for GNW/SNW!

The Notary Allies Client Intake Form is available on Kim Flanagan's website at https://www.notaryallies.com/specialty-general-notary-work. You can even put these pads on subscription and she'll deliver them on a regular schedule. You can also find a link to the form on the Readers Resource Website at www.NotaryCoach.com/90.

Date Completed:

Challenge Review

Notes or initial observations:

What worked:

What didn't work:

What will you continue to do?

What will you do differently next time?

DAY 39
UPLOAD ALL CONTACTS TO YOUR CRM

Today, we stop procrastinating.

Your challenge is to upload ALL of your contacts to your Customer Relationship Manager (CRM) tool or software.

You'll recall an earlier challenge was to do some research and purchase a CRM. That step alone was likely overwhelming, so good on you if you accomplished it.

And chances are, if you now have a CRM, it may not contain all of your contacts yet.

This downloading and uploading of contacts can cause us to freeze up sometimes.

Today, you figure it out.

Whichever CRM system you chose, it's time to take it on.

Visit the FAQ or the Help section and get the instructions for uploading your database.

Take a breath (or ten), grab a coffee or tea, and hunker down.

This may take some tinkering. Technology doesn't always work the way it's supposed to. But you'll get it.

Having your database of contacts in a CRM like this will make it much easier to stay in touch and deliver value.

We don't have to spend our lives scrambling for brand new customers all the time.

If our past customers needed a Notary once, they'll need one again. Or, they'll know someone who does.

If we stay in touch, we keep ourselves Top of Mind, so when they need a Notary, we're here.

This is important for next-level advancement. Invest the time today and watch your business blossom tomorrow.

NBB Resource: *The TOMM app allows for all of your contacts to be uploaded. You can bring them in individually, or you can do a mass transfer. Watch the video on the Readers Resource Website at www.NotaryCoach.com/90 to learn more.*

Date Completed:

Challenge Review

Notes or initial observations:

What worked:

What didn't work:

What will you continue to do?

What will you do differently next time?

DAY 40
TAKE A DISC ASSESSMENT

When you work in a people business like we do, it's important to understand how you're showing up to the world around you.

That means understanding the impact of your

- Words

- Tone

- Actions

- Facial expressions

This is all part of taking responsibility for our emotional wake—how we make people feel when we're interacting with them, or when we leave a room or conversation.

One of the things I learned from my friend and business-connection expert Nancy Patchak is that the "Golden Rule" of business is not always what associates are looking for.

"Treat me the way you would treat yourself" doesn't always work.

Instead, the Platinum Rule is far more effective:

"Treat me the way I want to be treated."

When you learn to communicate with people the way they prefer to be communicated with, the world opens up to you.

This is a fundamental foundation of the DiSC Personality Profile system.

That's why so many companies adopt the DiSC wisdom into their business and team development. It helps people communicate better . . . when it's used.

DiSC is based on four personality styles:

- D = Dominance

A person primarily in this DiSC quadrant places emphasis on accomplishing results and "seeing the big picture." They are confident, sometimes blunt, outspoken, and demanding.

- i = influence

A person in this quadrant places emphasis on relationships and on influencing or persuading others. They tend to be enthusiastic, optimistic, open, trusting, and energetic.

- S = Steadiness

A person in this quadrant places emphasis on cooperation, sincerity, loyalty, and dependability. They tend to have calm, deliberate dispositions, and don't like to be rushed.

- C = Conscientiousness

A person in this quadrant places emphasis on quality, accuracy, expertise, and competency. They enjoy their independence, demand the details, and often fear being wrong.

We each have a little of all four of these personality types, but we tend to "live" in one or two of them the majority of the time. Knowing where you fall in the DiSC profile is one more step toward self-awareness—understanding more about how you show up to the world.

As you dig even deeper into the styles, you'll be able to pick up hints from your direct escrow officers, attorneys, or even schedulers that can help you adapt your communication style to what serves the mission and moves you forward.

Your challenge today is to take the DiSC Profile Assessment and learn your unique behavioral style.

Like any assessment, there are free versions and paid versions online. I've tried all kinds of versions, but ultimately I prefer the OG when it comes to DiSC—the Everything DiSC, published by Wiley.

There's a small fee to take the assessment, but you get TONS of additional value with it, including an online account with practical resources and connection tools to help you implement your newfound knowledge of yourself.

You can find the Everything DiSC assessment on Catalyst when you visit https://www.realconnections2day.com/products/.

I land smack-dab in the middle of i and D; iD—perfect for a Notary. :-)

The cool thing about having your profile on Catalyst is we can share our profile information with each other, too.

Enjoy your journey into self!

Date Completed:

Challenge Review

Notes or initial observations:

What worked:

What didn't work:

What will you continue to do?

What will you do differently next time?

DAY 41
ADD 3 TO 5 CONTACTS TO YOUR DATABASE EVERY DAY

We've established how important it is to have a contact list, or a database, of your clients, friends, family, and prospects, right?

Your challenge today is to make a habit of adding three to five names to your contact list every day.

When you're in the hustle and bustle of your business, this is actually pretty easy. Everyone you meet for a Notary appointment, or any other service you provide, goes on your contact list.

If your service calls have dropped, or you're just getting started in this business, finding three to five people to add to your contacts each day becomes more of a challenge.

This is your time to shine, too.

FIND three to five people to talk to about your business OR theirs. (That's a huge OR. Think about how many people out there have a business they'd love to talk to you about).

Have conversations with everyone. Start with what and whom you know and may be comfortable with. Where are you going today in your errands? When people ask you what you do for a living, how do you answer? Start including "Mobile Notary and Loan Signing Agent" (or whatever title you LOVE) as part of that answer. That alone can spark a conversation.

Too shy?

Get a T-shirt or a car magnet made featuring your business. The conversation comes to you sometimes.

But don't stop with handing out a business card or simply answering questions.

Take control of the communication and get their contact info too. Even if they don't have a business card, get their name, phone number, and/or email address.

This is a critical step for staying in touch so you can share your value and allow your prospects to get to know you, like you, and trust you.

There's something bigger happening here than a simple sign, date, and stamp of a signature.

NBB Resource: *Members can explore the Morning Mastery and Daily Do's where I dive deeper into my use of the contact list, CRM, and staying in touch.*

Date Completed:

Challenge Review

Notes or initial observations:

What worked:

What didn't work:

What will you continue to do?

What will you do differently next time?

DAY 42
START A BUSINESS PAGE ON
LINKEDIN OR FACEBOOK

Let's talk about exposure.

Not the kind of exposure I get as a pasty ginger guy in the sun, but the good kind of exposure for your business.

Social media, whether we like it or not, can be beneficial for growing your network and sharing your passionate journey through this business.

LinkedIn is the clearly the online place where your ideal customers can be found. Earlier in the challenge, I tasked you to create your own LinkedIn personal profile page. That was for you, as an individual.

But did you know LinkedIn also offers a way to build a page for your business?

Today's challenge is to create a new business page for your services on Facebook or LinkedIn (or another platform you prefer).

This is only the first step, of course. Beyond setting up the page, you'll need to interact with it. But for now, let's focus on setting it up and using keywords to keep it semi-optimized.

Luckily, both Facebook and LinkedIn will practically take your hand and walk you through the set-up steps. And, if you've done your homework, or the work involved in this Notary Funnel Challenge, you should have some clarity on keywords, your ideal customers, and your full range of services to include as you build your business page.

Visit the Readers Resource Website for links to both LinkedIn and Facebook Business Page instructions: www.NotaryCoach.com/90.

I know what you're thinking . . .

"Bill, what if I want to set up a business page on both Facebook and LinkedIn?"

Permission granted! Do both!

Just remember that creating business pages isn't the magic wand that suddenly generates unlimited service calls and sales volume. There's more to the equation. Setting up a business page and just stopping there is like walking into a networking meeting and being tucked away in a corner like a fly on the wall. Sure, maybe someone will make their way over to you because you happen to be standing between them and the restroom (or the bar), but it's not an effective way to develop business.

Set up your page and work it.

- Write posts.

- Tag them.

- Share the passion you have for this business.

And, use your page as a platform to share your blogs, vlogs, and other valuable content.

People work with who they know, like, and trust.

THIS is how they get to know, like, and trust YOU.

Date Completed:

Challenge Review

Notes or initial observations:

What worked:

What didn't work:

What will you continue to do?

What will you do differently next time?

DAY 43
MEET A NOTARY FOR COFFEE

You're amazing.

How do I know that?

First, you're here, committed to making this business work and being of service as you do so.

Second, Notaries are special.

One of the greatest gifts of my life is to work within, and serve, this community. I know you likely feel the same.

Today's challenge is to meet a local Notary.

Set up an appointment for

- Coffee

- Tea

- Cocktails

- A walk

- A hike

- A kayak ride

- A Zoom?

- Whatever!

Just meet!

Get to know each other. Do you vibe? Do you not? (That's okay too!)

You won't know until you meet up and see what they're made of. Sometimes we're in alignment with others and sometimes we aren't.

No judgment either way.

Still, it's important to reach out and connect.

See how you can support each other.

One of my favorite questions to ask during meetings like this is "How can I support you right now?"

See where that takes you.

If you don't know where to find Notaries in your area, pretend you are a customer in need of a Notary. Google "Notary Near Me" and start there. What kind of results pop up? LOTS of profiles. Read them. Find out who resonates with you, or who you relate to by the words they use or experience they have. Pay attention to how they answer the phone, IF they answer the phone. Keep going until you find "your person." They're out there.

Date Completed:

Challenge Review

Notes or initial observations:

What worked:

What didn't work:

What will you continue to do?

What will you do differently next time?

DAY 44
SEND A NOTE OF CONGRATULATIONS TO SOMEONE DESERVING

What a gift we have to act on our promptings and do good work.

Your challenge today is to send a note of congratulations or goodwill to someone who is celebrating something special.

How do you know who is celebrating?

In today's world, they are likely sharing it on social media.

Start there. It's easy. And when you're starting a new habit, easy is helpful.

Scroll through your Facebook, Instagram, or LinkedIn feed and find someone celebrating an anniversary, a promotion, a vacation, a birth, a new pet, a book launch, a course creation—SOMETHING.

Then, send them a nice note honoring them and the occasion.

Consider sending the note in a more personal format than just commenting on a post. Commenting is still good, but go deeper in a private message, a text, a phone call, or even a handwritten note or card.

I think you'll find that celebrating the victories of others can be a joyful practice for you.

Making a habit out of something as simple as this practice can enhance the lives of those in your network, and your own.

This doesn't have to be limited to work associates. Friends and family count too! Facebook does a great job of reminding you about birthdays, and you may even have an old address book or calendar you use for anniversaries and birthdays. This is your chance to be the person in your network who seems to remember everything!

Date Completed:

Challenge Review

Notes or initial observations:

What worked:

What didn't work:

What will you continue to do?

What will you do differently next time?

DAY 45
BUILD YOUR ADVISORY BOARD

Whom do you go to for trusted counsel?

My friend Greg Reid proposes that there's a huge difference between the good counsel we need and the opinions we often get. Counsel is typically based on wisdom, knowledge, and experience. Opinions are based on observation and judgment.

Read Greg's article in *Rolling Stone* here:

https://www.rollingstone.com/culture-council/articles/outside-counsel-not-opinions-1183899/.

Here's the thing: You won't have just ONE person who can provide counsel on all aspects of life and business. It's going to take a team.

Your challenge today is to start building your Advisory Board.

Who belongs on your Advisory Board?

Well, first, remember this is YOUR business and YOU get to decide. No rules, baby!

And second, here are some suggestions for advisors who made all the difference to me:

- Certified Public Accountant WITH entrepreneur experience. (If they've never owned a business, the conversation and experience is VERY different.)

- Financial/investment advisor WITH entrepreneur experience or perspective. (Life is different for us, and you need someone who thinks beyond a 401K.)

- Micro-niche coaches and mentors. (Find a laser-focused coach when you need one; those focused on copywriting, course creation, and book publishing are a few I chose. You may choose an apostille agent or wedding officiant or people focused on loan signing, fingerprinting, etc.)

- General business coach. (Make sure they *know* business.)

- Therapist or counselor. (There is no difference between you and your business as a solo-preneur. Personal baggage becomes work baggage.)

- Specialized investment advisor. (Find a real estate expert, a retail expert, a business-buying expert, or whatever. Get micro-niche advice here too.)

- Various attorneys. (This is why I love LegalShield. Whether landlord/tenant, incorporation, estate planning, copyright infringement, or another specialty, I have an expert at my fingertips. One way or another, you'll need specific legal counsel.)

- Real estate agent. (A great real estate agent provides counsel and seasoned advice on decisions you need to make.)

- Loan officer. (Again, you're not looking for a salesperson here. You're looking for an advisor who will guide you to the right decision EVEN if it means not refinancing or buying.)

- Medical team advisors. (Find skilled physicians, nurse practitioners, health coaches, etc.)

- Fitness coaches. (Hire a respected personal trainer, yogi, nutritionist, etc.)

- Spiritual advisor. (Connect with a member of the clergy, or someone else you trust along your spiritual journey.)

There's a really good chance you have some candidates for these advisory positions in your network already. Without intention, though, they often slip into ambiguity and are easily forgotten.

As part of your challenge today, make a list of potential Advisory Board members for all endeavors.

Then, set up some conversations. These can be on the phone, Zoom, email, or in person.

You get to interview them a bit.

They'll do the same with you.

Here's what that might look like:

"Jack, I run a small business and I am building a team of advisors to help me get to the next level. Can we schedule some time to chat about how we might support each other in this?"

That's it.

Be straight up with where you're at and where you're going.

You'll find people you immediately connect with and you'll know they're a good fit for your team.

And likewise, you'll know who isn't (often before the meeting even starts).

Build your Advisory Board with those who fit, then make an effort to stay in touch and seek their good counsel—even if you have to pay for it. It's an investment your business can't afford to miss.

Date Completed:

Challenge Review

Notes or initial observations:

What worked:

What didn't work:

What will you continue to do?

What will you do differently next time?

DAY 46
OFFICE POP-INS

Here we go stretching the comfort zone again.

Today's challenge is to schedule a "Pop-in," as described by friend and NBB cofounder Jennifer Neitzel.

Pop-ins are a way to engage with prospective clients in person by swinging by their office with a little gift or simply introducing yourself and proposing a conversation.

First, prepare for your pop-in. Would you like to drop off a little gift? Pens? Sticky notes? Holiday-specific doodads?

Second, do some research ahead of time. Where do you want to go? Whom do you want to meet and talk to? What are they up to?

Third, pop in! Introduce yourself and see if you can get some face time with the person you decided you wanted to meet.

Fourth, whether you got some face time or not, plan your follow-up. Thank them for their time, or discreetly check in on the gifts you left behind.

Fifth, follow up again. And again. And again.

The fortune is in the follow-up.

Jennifer Neitzel teaches her highly effective approach to office pop-ins and more in her wonderful program "Signing Agent Marketing" (find it at https://www.signingagentmarketing.com/), as well as in her live classes within Notary Business Builder at https://www.notarycoach.com/nbbfresh. In NBB, she teaches the integration of TOMM and automated follow-up with email campaigns and more. Join NBB today at a discounted rate at the link above.

Date Completed:

Challenge Review

Notes or initial observations:

What worked:

What didn't work:

What will you continue to do?

What will you do differently next time?

DAY 47
JOIN THE CHAMBER OF COMMERCE

Your local community is eager to support you.

And, equally so, you can support them. Your services are necessary for just about everyone in your city.

How powerful is that?

It's not often we get to embark in a business where our customers will be required to need our services at some point.

That doesn't mean we get to be lackadaisical about our business. Customers still have a choice in whom they hire. And community involvement makes a difference to many.

It's time to get dialed in.

Your challenge today is to explore membership in your local Chamber of Commerce OR other local civic organizations.

My friend and fellow NBB cofounder Laura Biewer enjoyed being on the ribbon-cutting committee of her local chamber. It gave her access to new businesses and a reason to celebrate with fellow entrepreneurs.

Many of these civic organizations have similar committees.

We often gain the most support by supporting others. Funny how that works.

Date Completed:

Challenge Review

Notes or initial observations:

What worked:

What didn't work:

What will you continue to do?

What will you do differently next time?

DAY 48
CHECK YOUR WEBSITE FOR COMMON ERRORS

This might be a light day for you.

Your challenge today is to check your website for the most common mistakes Notaries make.

This is easy if you received good counsel when your website went up in the first place, OR if you don't have a website yet (which, of course, is a whole different conversation).

But I know how it goes when you're starting a business. Sometimes it's a hodge-podge of all the essential ingredients of a business, such as having a website, often slapped together until we have time to revisit and enhance.

Today's the day!

Revisit and enhance your website.

I wrote an article that can help guide you through the journey titled "The 11 Biggest Notary Website Mistakes and How to Avoid Them," based on a webinar we did with my friend and fellow NBB faculty member Tyler Botsford, a digital marketing expert.

Read the article here: https://www.notarycoach.com/blog/seo.

The article goes into a lot more detail, but here are the **11 biggest website mistakes to look out for and avoid**:

1. Not optimizing your website

2. Not having a website at all!

3. Bad/confusing website design/user experience

4. Difficult to remember URLs (web addresses)

5. Not identifying your keywords

6. Nonresponsive or nonmobile-friendly site

7. Not having a call to action (CTA)

8. No SSL certificate

9. No credentials, certifications, or social proof on your site

10. Not listing your additional services

11. Too much text and no photos

Remember, you're in a safe place here. It's a judgment-free zone. Don't shame yourself if you find a few or more of these mistakes on your website. You did the best you could at the time. Now you know, and it's easy to adjust. So adjust. Get to work!

Challenge Review

Notes or initial observations:

What worked:

What didn't work:

What will you continue to do?

What will you do differently next time?

DAY 49
SPONSOR AN EVENT

Sponsoring events can be a great way to support your local community AND give your business exceptional exposure.

Today's challenge is to find a local event, team, or performance to sponsor.

Opportunities abound here.

Personally, I love this gift of being in business. Truthfully, if I could spend my life sponsoring creative and heart-filled projects, it's exactly what I would do. Interestingly, being a business owner provides these opportunities every day.

Here are some ideas for sponsorship:

- Youth sports teams. (Start with your family and work outward.)

- Civic events. (Through Chamber of Commerce, Kiwanis, Rotary, etc.)

- Industry events. (Think bar associations, NNA conference, Notary symposium, divorce professionals, international adoption associations, teacher associations, etc.).

- LinkedIn local events

- Networking events

- Breakfast meetings, etc.

- Conventions, conferences, and workshops in various niche markets

Sponsorship of events like these rarely results in immediate returns but does create exposure, name recognition, and good will. Sponsorship is a long-term investment, so set your sites on being of service and supporting the organization at hand.

If possible, plan on more than one event; maybe sponsor a series.

Stay as engaged as possible if you're going to invest in this. A logo on a banner doesn't do the trick. People work with who they know, like, and trust. Be involved. Your logo and banner should remind people of your greatness. It should not be relied upon to establish it.

So reach out! Explore and discover your sponsorship opportunities right now.

Your network is the perfect place to start . . .

Date Completed:

Challenge Review

Notes or initial observations:

What worked:

What didn't work:

What will you continue to do?

What will you do differently next time?

DAY 50
ENHANCE YOUR LINKEDIN HEADLINE

You've hung in here this long. We're now over half the way through the Notary Funnel Challenge.

Let's say we DO THIS!

Your LinkedIn headline is like a magnet for your ideal customer. Let's make sure you're attracting what you want.

Today's challenge is to enhance your LinkedIn headline to match your desires.

The LinkedIn headline allows you 220 characters to describe your value to the exact people who will need your services.

THIS is worth your attention.

The LinkedIn headline is more than a simple job title such as Notary Public.

Use the headline to describe more of the value you bring to the table.

THIS is where you want to be all extra about it.

At the very least, write something like "Mobile Notary and Loan Signing Agent | A Notary Who Comes to YOU on Your Schedule | Apostille Agent Expedited Services | Full-Service Credentialed Professional Specializing in Senior Services | [etc.]"

Tell them what you want them to know in the first few seconds.

How do you solve problems?

That's what your headline is all about. And think about it from their perspective and experience, not yours. What do your potential clients need and want? Speak to that, and show some personality that is all your own.

You won't go wrong.

And please, let's connect on LinkedIn. Send me a message or follow me here: https://www.linkedin.com/in/billsoroka/.

NBB Resource: *NBB members get exclusive access to LinkedIn consultant and trainer Sandra Long's course, "LinkedIn Professional Profile," which walks you through the entire profile set-up process so you can take full advantage of all the tools available on LinkedIn.*

Date Completed:

Challenge Review

Notes or initial observations:

What worked:

What didn't work:

What will you continue to do?

What will you do differently next time?

DAY 51
CREATE A CUSTOM URL FOR YOUR REVIEWS

I know I am preaching to the choir.

- Customer reviews matter.

- You have to ask for them.

- You must make it easy for them to deliver.

Capisce (Capeesh)?

We're 51 days into this Notary Funnel Challenge and I know that you know you have to get serious about diversification and your Google Business Profile. Reviews make a huge difference there.

Your challenge today is to create a custom URL to direct your customers to for giving a review.

Let's make it easy for you AND your clients to remember your customer review link.

This is SO easy!

First, decide where you want your customers to leave a review. For most of us, that will be on Google Business Profile (see the importance here???).

Then, choose a domain name that makes sense for your personal brand or business. A domain name is the "address" you'll give clients, like www.amazingreviewsofmynotaryservicesandmore.com (except NEVER choose a domain that long). Make it easy to remember, like "MyNotaryReviews" or "411NotaryReviews" or "AZNotaryReviews." You get to decide; it's YOUR business!

Then you forward your new domain to your review location, and your clients can easily post your reviews for the world to see.

Get creative and have fun!

I use GoDaddy to buy all my domains. These cost a maximum of $20 per year, and are often much less if you're new to them. The process to forward domains is, well, straightforward, and GoDaddy offers excellent customer support.

Date Completed:

Challenge Review

Notes or initial observations:

What worked:

What didn't work:

What will you continue to do?

What will you do differently next time?

DAY 52
FORGIVE YOURSELF AND OTHERS

It's time to let go.

In today's challenge, I encourage you to forgive yourself and others by creating a daily (or regular) forgiveness ritual.

We get hurt. A lot, actually.

Especially when you're in business. If you stick your neck out, there is bound to be an axe.

Still, there's no power in clinging to victimhood, resentment, and pain in the long term.

I default to those much wiser than I: **"Resentment (or hatred, or anger) is like taking poison and waiting for the other person to die."**

Sometimes we get hurt on purpose. Sometimes by accident.

We also sometimes hurt others. Sometimes on purpose, and sometimes by accident. We're complicated beings.

Either way, this can really jam things up for us.

It's time to learn from the experience, clean things up, and do better next time.

One of the rituals I incorporated into my life helps clear the energy.

Every night before I got to bed, I recite the following:

"Knowing that forgiveness is the key to unconditional love and the experience of spiritual power, I now forgive anyone and everyone who has ever injured me in any way, real or imagined. I let go of the mistaken idea that anyone's actions have the power to diminish my light or my life. I now also forgive myself for any shortcomings or mistaken judgments and their resulting effects."

I learned this from a spiritual mastermind many years ago. It helps me come to terms with both the outer AND the inner critic, and I sleep better at night.

I hope it helps you too.

Date Completed:

Challenge Review

Notes or initial observations:

What worked:

What didn't work:

What will you continue to do?

What will you do differently next time?

DAY 53
SET UP YOUR GOOGLE BUSINESS PROFILE

Before I announce today's challenge, I have a question for you:

Do you want more general or specialty Notary work outside of loan signings?

If your answer is no, then I would still encourage you to do today's challenge, but also to figure out how you will diversify your revenue streams.

If your answer is yes, you DO want more GNW/SNW, then today's challenge is your top priority.

Your challenge is to start, or claim, your Google Business Profile (GBP) page, if you haven't already.

GBP is a free suite of services offered by Google to help local businesses get found on the Google search engine.

Yup, free.

And, in case you didn't know it yet, nearly every consumer who is your potential customer is looking for your services online with Google. And 94% of them use the Reviews feature to help make their final hiring decisions.

See, this is important.

I know you likely have three big concerns about this:

1. The expense

2. The technology

3. The privacy

I addressed the expense earlier. This service is FREE.

I have a solution for the technology piece for you below. Jim Allen, the Marketing Notary, provided a free tutorial training that walks you through claiming your GBP step by step. It's a replay of an event from late June 2022. Use it if you'd like some help.

And when it comes to privacy, many people are concerned with having to put their address into Google Business Profiles. Rarely do we want strangers knocking on our door for Notary services. This is NOT required. You can hide your address from the public and still have an effective profile. Jim will show you how in the training.

So there you have it.

GBP takes some time to gain speed and impact, so get started today. These are the seeds of trees of business for tomorrow and the years to come.

You can watch the training replay featuring Jim Allen on "Claiming (and Starting) Your Google Business Profile" on the Readers Resource Website at www.NotaryCoach.com/90.

Date Completed:

Challenge Review

Notes or initial observations:

What worked:

What didn't work:

What will you continue to do?

What will you do differently next time?

DAY 54
CREATE AN ONLINE GROUP
FOR IDEAL CLIENTS

What if you created a space for your ideal customers?

Today's challenge is to create a Facebook or LinkedIn group (or Circle group, Mighty Networks group, etc.) that caters to and attracts those whom YOU have decided are your ideal customers.

Using such groups to provide value to your customers is a powerful way to establish yourself as an expert, a thought leader, and an excellent practitioner as a mobile Notary and loan signing agent (and beyond).

Here's what this might look like. Remember, there are no rules and this is YOUR business:

Let's say you have decided that you love working with Family Law attorneys who specialize in prenuptial agreements, adoptions, estate planning, and even divorce.

You could start a semi-private Facebook or LinkedIn Group called, "Chicago-Area All Things Family Law & Estate Planning Networking Group."

Set up your group rules. Facebook has a template for this, and you can adjust it as you wish.

Use the Questions feature to pre-screen people for the group. You want quality over quantity in these things. Let attorneys, estate planning reps, paralegals, appraisers, legal document preparers, etc., join the group and encourage them to add value (not advertise). That usually means sharing resources and wisdom.

Be sure you stay active in your own group too. Introduce yourself, provide value, lead discussions. Poll your members.

The key to success in leveraging these online groups is to be crystal clear and refined in your definition of the ideal customer. Remember, with clarity comes customers.

And the second important key is to stimulate group engagement with value, NOT ADVERTISING. If you or other members of the group just consistently "hunt" prospects, your potential clients will leave. Remember, these top performers have dreams of their own, and they're looking for connections and value too.

Third, avoid being too "on the nose" with your group name. "Sacramento Notary Services Group" won't likely attract attorneys. Maybe other Notaries, so if that's your target audience, great. But think from your ideal customers' perspective. What do they need or want? How can you help them succeed? Build a group around those answers and you'll have yourself a home run.

Date Completed:

Challenge Review

Notes or initial observations:

What worked:

What didn't work:

What will you continue to do?

What will you do differently next time?

DAY 55
EVALUATE YOUR JOURNALING PROCESS

Today involves a little more quiet reflection within the Notary Funnel Challenge.

Your challenge is to evaluate your personal Notary journaling process.

This evaluation is part of Kaizen, the philosophy and practice of continuous improvement through regular small, incremental changes. *Every* appointment gives us the opportunity to refine our processes as Notaries.

I'd be remiss if I didn't say this first: Even if your state does not require a Notary Journal, you absolutely SHOULD be using a Notary Journal. This journal acts as your memory should any of your transactions be challenged later down the road. And let's face it, by even having a document notarized in the first place, someone is anticipating a problem down the road. Why else take the time to prove it was signed by the principal?

USE A JOURNAL.

And now that I know most of you are already using a journal, let's talk about what it is you are evaluating as part of today's challenge.

Review your state statutes, specifically the section where they discuss journal requirements. Are you in compliance? If not, adjust accordingly now. Don't worry about fixing the past. If your state does not require a journal, you can approach journaling any way you want. You can read up on best practices in the book *Professor Closen's Notary Best Practices*, by Michael Closen.

Review efficiency. How is the journal process working for you? Is it jamming up your appointments or is it part of your workflow? If it's jammed up, where is the clog? Are you using the right journal in the first place? If not, try a new one. In most states you can terminate the use of a journal at any time. The time lost and frustration you experience in the meantime is worth far more than the $15 to $50 or so it costs for a new journal.

I currently recommend each of these three journals:

- *The Notary eJournal* (electronic journal with digital fingerprint technology): https://www.notarycoach.com/ejournal

- *Integrity Notary Journal*: https://mobilenotarykc.com/integrity-journal

- *Notary Ally Journal:* https://www.notaryallies.com/loan-signing-agents-options

Every appointment is an opportunity to refine your processes and your flow. Each and every day you get better and better.

Date Completed:

Challenge Review

Notes or initial observations:

What worked:

What didn't work:

What will you continue to do?

What will you do differently next time?

DAY 56
PRACTICE CONNECTING WITHOUT
SELLING YOUR SERVICES

Your challenge today is to practice connecting with an ideal customer without selling your services in the first few messages.

This is both a skill and an art form that requires attention and constant practice.

It's a bit ironic because most of us don't want to be "that guy"—you know, the one who only reaches out when he or she has something to sell, without regard to our own well-being, interests, or journey. And yet . . . many of us end up doing exactly that, and more often than not, we start off a new relationship this way.

Our first message to new contacts is verbal vomit about how amazing our services are and how much E&O insurance we have.

Been there. Done that.

I've made this mistake ON REPEAT.

It's easy to justify being in a hurry, or "not beating around the bush."

But that's a cop-out.

We're in a relationship-based business, and relationships take time. And, they're worth the extra time and effort to show you care about the other person, not just their business.

So do this instead:

- Using LinkedIn as an example, because most of your ideal customers can be found there, find someone you have on your Fab 100 list—a person you want to work with or connect with, but haven't yet.

- Using the 2 in 5 strategy, spend five minutes reviewing that person's profile. Look at content they've created, liked, or commented on. See where they work. Read their About section. Find two things that jump out as interesting to you.

- Use the Connect feature to connect, and do so with a message. That means you may have to use the three little dots, or Follow them first. Keep your message short and sweet and try to incorporate the one or two things you learned about them during the 2 in 5 exercise.

Your message might say something like one of these:

"Hey Roger—It's such a small world; I went to Trenton High as well! It's great to see you absolutely killing it in your business. I work in the peripheral of real estate as well and would love to stay in touch."

"Hi Cindy—I just saw that you run a wine and cheese networking event in Scottsdale each month and it sounds amazing. Let's connect so we can stay in touch. I'd love to learn more!"

"Good day, Lois! It's quite clear from your content that you love helping seniors thrive. I wish my grandparents had found you earlier! I too am passionate about helping the community and I'd love to connect and see if there is a way we can support each other in business."

You can start a conversation like this any number of ways, depending on what people share and how you relate to it. Have fun. Be authentic. And don't sell anything.

Try it on one person today.

Date Completed:

Challenge Review

Notes or initial observations:

What worked:

What didn't work:

What will you continue to do?

What will you do differently next time?

DAY 57
START A YOUTUBE CHANNEL

Today, we explore the power of video.

Creating videos with content that can help your ideal customers is one of the fastest ways to grow your reputation and allow your audience to get to know, like, and trust you.

Yes, even as a solo Notary in your city, making videos can enhance your business. You don't have to be a trainer or a mentor to capitalize on the value of videos.

There are actually several ways to do this these days:

- TikTok

- Facebook stories

- Instagram stories and reels
  (See https://www.demandsage.com/instagram-reels-vs-stories/ for a comparison.)

- LinkedIn videos

- YouTube

And even more!

I'm going to talk most specifically about YouTube today because Google owns it. And guess what? Google loves Google. So YouTube videos are likely to get ranked toward the top of your potential customer's Google searches.

So, if someone in your city searches for "How to get an apostille in Michigan" and you have a video called "How to Get an Apostille in Michigan," do you know what pops up for them? YOUR video!

If you pack that video full of value, showing some personality along with helpful hints, and include a specific call to action for those who need more help, you've likely got yourself a new customer.

Your challenge today is to start your own YouTube channel.

Don't stress about content, makeup, hairstyle, backgrounds, or cameras just yet. Simply start your channel.

You can find the technical steps to create your YouTube Channel here: https://support.google.com/youtube/answer/1646861?hl=en

Having a YouTube channel will be an exercise in constant refinement (yet again!). Done is better than perfect.

If you want to take on your YouTube art right away, Canva has templates pre-built for this.

Okay, producer, get to creating your channel!

NBB Resource: *When it comes to creating content for your YouTube channel, NBB members have lots of resources with the full "Get Known Strategy" course that is included. Get topic ideas, learn the basics of video production, and most importantly, learn how to distribute your content via social media and email.*

Date Completed:

Challenge Review

Notes or initial observations:

What worked:

What didn't work:

What will you continue to do?

What will you do differently next time?

DAY 58
OPTIMIZE YOUR DIRECTORY LISTINGS

Let's take a look at those directory listings.

As we discussed in the Day 37 Challenge, there are plenty of free Notary directories out there, and some of them offer "premium" listings for a fee.

Whether or not you've paid for your listings, if you want them to perform and actually drive customers to you, you have to make sure they're optimized to do so.

Your challenge today is to optimize your online directory listings.

Start with one listing only; otherwise this can get overwhelming quickly.

I recommend you begin with your LinkedIn profile (your master profile), but a close second would be your SigningAgent.com listing. Apply the following optimization techniques to ONE of these profiles first, and then you can easily copy and paste the resulting content into your other profiles.

Here are a few ways you can optimize your profile:

- You must use a great photo of you, like a headshot. Do not use a logo. Do not use a photo of your dog. Use a recent photo you love—one that's up close and personal.

- Reveal a little of your personality, humor, or motivation behind your work behaviors. Are you quirky? Serious? Fun? Playful. Let it out here.

- Along the same lines, show your passion. Whom do you love to work with and why? What makes you special?

- Use the keywords associated with the ideal customers you hope to attract. Think of the document names they need notarized, or the specific services or specialties they would request. Or, what they'll be typing into Google when they are on the prowl for your services.

- My friend and fellow YouTuber, Seben "Griff" Griffin, shares a great idea about proactively addressing pain points of hiring companies. Let them know you are a pro and know what you're doing. "I understand the importance of printing docs on properly sized paper." Or, "I show up to every appointment on time, with clear communication, and in professional attire to represent you well at the closing table." Or, "I've completed over 5,000 loan signings up to my clients' standards and I am 100% coachable for yours too."

- Finally, where you have room and enough characters to do so, share more of your story. People like to work with who they know, like, and trust. Show them why you are the Notary they should choose. Make your first paragraph the one that answers all the questions and provides the info above. That's the one you can copy and paste into other profiles. Then, the longer narrative can be shared where it fits.

- Make sure your name, addresses, and phone numbers (NAP) match exactly on all profiles. This is surprisingly important for SEO purposes.

Way to get optimized!

Date Completed:

Challenge Review

Notes or initial observations:

What worked:

What didn't work:

What will you continue to do?

What will you do differently next time?

DAY 59
ANSWER THE PHONE PROFESSIONALLY

How do you answer your business phone line?

This is often how you make your first impression with a prospective customer and it can set the tone for your entire relationship . . . or lack thereof.

Today's challenge is to be intentional and professional when you answer the phone.

I wish the instructions for how to answer the phone were super simple. I mean, it is a simple thing, but there is definitely more to it than just choosing the right words to say.

Your attitude toward service calls in the first place makes a huge difference. As does your belief in what you're creating with each phone call.

There's something bigger happening here. Again, the way you answer your phone is often the very first impression potential customers have of you.

Here are some considerations for answering your business line:

- Be in proximity of your phone during business hours. Every time that phone rings, it's lifeblood for your business. No customers, no revenue. No revenue, no business.

- Answer with a professional greeting like "Speedy Notary, this is Bill. How can I help you?" or "Good Morning, this is Bill the Notary. How can I help?" Even a simple, "Hello, this is Bill," is better than, "Hello?" Just "Hello" is for personal lines. And even that seems antiquated and absurd to me these days with caller ID and contacts in our phone. The first words out of your mouth should demonstrate to the person on the other end of the line that they have a pro on the phone who is eager to serve.

- Use a tone of voice that suggests you actually want to help. Look, it's easy to get jaded in this business. We get inundated with calls from signing services that continue to lowball orders, or we get calls from the general public that pummel us about the cost of our services. Yes, those things happen, AND there are also plenty of people out there who value the real service we provide in this convenience economy. Don't turn off your ideal customer because you're exhausted or burned out from the other calls. Every caller has the chance to be a lifetime customer. Have reverence for that every time the phone rings.

- If you're too distracted to be warm, friendly, and present for the caller, either don't pick up at all, or pick up the call and ask them to please hold (and then mute your phone line on your mobile device) until you can get to a place where you can give them your full attention. Even if it means getting their name and number to call them right back. Trust me, this is better than ordering a cheeseburger at the drive-through, or angrily returning a torn pair of jeans at Target, with the customer on the line. Yep, both have happened to me while I was trying to hire a Notary for a gig.

Have a sales process and framework for every GNW/SNW call so you ask the right questions, set proper expectations, demonstrate your expertise, be a resource, and close the deal (set the appointment).

There you go! Five ways to set a good first impression right from the get-go.

Date Completed:

Challenge Review

Notes or initial observations:

What worked:

What didn't work:

What will you continue to do?

What will you do differently next time?

DAY 60
HAVE A CLEAR CTA ON YOUR WEBSITE

Let's avoid one of the most common mistakes Notaries make on their websites.

Today's challenge is to make sure your website has a clear Call to Action (CTA).

Your call to action is exactly that: What action do you want people to take when they are on your website?

Do you want them to:

- Call you?

- Text you?

- Email you?

- Book you online?

- Download information?

- Buy something?

Make sure your CTA is crystal clear to someone who has never been to your website before. And, make sure it is listed in more than one place, and at least one location is "above the fold" on your home page. That means a clear CTA should be featured on the home page toward the top, without requiring the customer to scroll down to find it.

Here are examples of clear call-to-action language that respond to your objectives above:

- Call me at 555-555-5555.

- Text me your questions at 555-555-5555.

- Email us at thebest@notaryboss.com.

- Schedule Your Notary Appointment Online Here!

- Download a free report on how virtual notarization can work for you.

- Buy Now!

When it comes to your website, think from your customers' perspective, not yours. Customers are often confused because they're not sure exactly what they need (some person or some document just said, "Sign in front of a Notary"), and they are used to immediate gratification. Don't make them hunt down your contact information. Make it easy to take action on every page of your website.

Date Completed:

Challenge Review

Notes or initial observations:

What worked:

What didn't work:

What will you continue to do?

What will you do differently next time?

DAY 61
CREATE A GRAPHIC USING CANVA

Did you set up your free Canva account yet?

As explained earlier, Canva is an online design and publishing tool you can use to easily create graphics to support your business. You can create social media images including LinkedIn and Facebook banners, posters, business cards, and much more!

Today, your challenge is to create a new graphic for your business.

Relax and have some fun with this. You get to choose what kind of graphic you want to create, and you DO NOT need to start from scratch. Canva offers you numerous templates that are easy to customize to your needs.

If you're like me, sometimes browsing Canva's templates will get your wheels turning and you'll come up with your best ideas while looking at their stuff.

That's okay!

- Jump into Canva.com now.

- If you haven't already, set up your free account. (I pay for the premium account and it has been worth every penny, but there's no pressure to do so.)

- On the left side of the screen, click on "Templates."

- You'll see all the different categories they offer, and you can choose any that call to you. Then, simply browse their templates and see what ideas may come to you.

- These are yours to use! Make quick edits to make sure they reflect your brand and your business, but Canva expects, and wants, you to use these for your business.

PS Want a wider selection of free photos for your graphics? Check out Unsplash at https://unsplash.com for stock photos that you can download for free. You can then use the upload feature in Canva to incorporate the photos into your beautiful graphics.

Date Completed:

Challenge Review

Notes or initial observations:

What worked:

What didn't work:

What will you continue to do?

What will you do differently next time?

DAY 62
SUNDAY SUCCESS RITUAL

I'm going to share a game-changing habit with you.

My Sunday Success Ritual helps me gain peace of mind while keeping me fired up and engaged with my goals.

Every Sunday, I practice a string of habits, often called a routine or a ritual, that celebrates, assesses, and plans, so that I walk into the week ahead with confidence, joy, and peace.

Your challenge today is to create a Sunday Success Ritual of your own.

I'll share a synopsis of my own ritual down below. For now, I want you to know how important this is. It's next level, and very few people do it. But top performers do. So you get to decide today: Are you a high performer ready for the next level? Or are you comfortable where you are, maintaining the status quo?

You're here, in the Notary Funnel Challenge, so I already know your answer. Are you ready to own it?

I like to block out two hours for my Sunday Success Ritual.

Sometimes it takes that long, but usually not. I like to leave time for the magic to happen. I encourage you to do the same. Just because a task is a habit, or part of a string of habits, doesn't mean you have to perform them like a machine. It's not all about outcomes or results. You have to allow for some time for you to become who you need to become in the process. These tasks, when done consciously and with intention, will push your boundaries and create a pathway for growth.

Plus, when you're moving forward on dreams that light you up from the inside, you may "spin out" in a daydream (or six) as you plan the week ahead. For me, that means I am enjoying the process. "*In-Joy-In* the process." Isn't that what it's all about? That means I am on track. That means I am living a life of purpose and I am in alignment with my bigger dreams.

Leave some time and space for you to feel that as you build your Sunday Success Ritual.

Here's an overview of my personal Sunday Success Ritual:

- Start by celebrating five or six of your wins from the last week. Write those down. Celebrate the big wins, the small wins, and everything in between. This was a huge lesson for me. I used to skip on to the next endeavor, project, or goal without slowing down to savor the journey and acknowledge the process. This portion of the Sunday Success Ritual gives me permission and space to do so.

- Take a look at your goals from last week. How'd you do? Make progress toward them or complete them? Remember, this is not an exercise in shame (or excuses, for that matter). You're the only one who will read this, so don't BS yourself. And don't get down on yourself, either! Everything is negotiable.

- Think through your previous week. What worked for you? Did you find a new route? A new process? A new way of saying something or describing a document? Write that down! Conversely, what didn't work for you last week? Did you come across a document you weren't aware of? A Notarial act that stumped you? Is sleeping in until 8 a.m. not working for you anymore? Make a note!

- Look at the week ahead, day by day. What's coming up? What do you need to do to prepare for those events? Schedule the preparation AND the follow-up. Like, literally, schedule it. Make an appointment on your calendar to do the work. This simple process right here can end the last-minute scurry to complete PowerPoints for meetings, send follow-up info, and more. What gets scheduled, gets done!

- Schedule your self-care too. This can't be all about business. That's easy to forget in this field, especially when you love what you do. We tend to work, and work, and work, and work . . . But in order to help the most people, you have to put on your own oxygen mask first. Schedule your walks, your gym time, your meal prep, your playtime with the kids—everything.

- Be gentle with yourself. As I said above, everything is negotiable. If you come across an appointment you set for yourself and with yourself, and something else comes up, or you're just out of energy, don't get down on yourself. Be kind to you. And reschedule it. That's not a lack of integrity. Integrity is renegotiating previous agreements. If you scheduled some time to write your book in the morning, but your partner suggests a hand-in-hand walk to pick up breakfast groceries, do that instead. Don't skip the writing and berate yourself, creating resentment in both you and your spouse; rather, reschedule it. Be aware of the conversation in your mind as you do so. You're witnessing a becoming process right there.

- And finally, choose three to five goals for next week. These should be in alignment with annual or quarterly goals, meaning that by accomplishing the coming week's goals, you'll be propelled toward the higher vision. These will be your top three to five priorities for the week.

- Dissect and schedule your top three to five goals. Depending on what the goals are, you may need to complete some specific tasks before those goals can be accomplished. Reverse-engineer each goal and schedule the tasks that have to be done in order to accomplish the goal. Remember, what gets scheduled, gets done.

You can probably see why I block out a couple hours to complete my ritual every week. It's important and it's comprehensive.

I landed on this after years of chasing "quick" goal-planning alternatives.

"They" sell us quick fixes because that's what we respond to at a lower level of ourselves. We don't need quick. Quick is fine if it works, but too often quick means shallow.

These are our frickin' dreams we're talking about here. This is our life, right here and right now. We need depth.

Go deep for your dreams. Spend some time spinning them to life on a Sunday morning or afternoon. Keep yourself connected and always moving toward them.

THAT is a Sunday Success Ritual.

Date Completed:

Challenge Review

Notes or initial observations:

What worked:

What didn't work:

What will you continue to do?

What will you do differently next time?

DAY 63
CREATE A PROFESSIONAL EMAIL ADDRESS

I actually had an escrow client who immediately deleted inquiries from notaries with an AOL email account because she said it demonstrated lack of technology experience.

Many other escrow clients I've worked with also often disregard personal email addresses from Yahoo, Hotmail, and even Gmail accounts if the addresses don't look professional enough.

They assume these Notaries just aren't serious about their businesses.

Weird, right?

Accurate? Well, I don't know.

But here's the thing: In business, it doesn't matter if it's accurate because perception is reality. If your potential clients think your email address is unprofessional, then it is. Done deal. You can't argue it in front of Judge Judy.

We can't control everything, of course, but there are some ways we can grab the reins and represent our brand in the best way possible. Your email address is one such way.

Your challenge today is to create a professional email address.

A professional email address is typically one that uses a custom domain for your business or brand.

This is opposed to an email address that uses @gmail, @yahoo, @ymail, and definitely @aol (sorry!).

It may seem cheap and easy to simply use an email address like GloriousGadfordGeorgiaLoanSigningAgentExtraordinaire@gmail.com, but it's probably costing you business.

You can easily get an email address that uses your website domain. Sometimes this is included with the cost of the website and sometimes it may cost a small fee.

For instance, you can always find me at Bill@NotaryCoach.com.

I own the domain NotaryCoach.com.

Then, I pay Google Workspace a few bucks a month to let me use Bill@ as my email address.

I also have Orders@.

And Notary@.

Well, you get it.

Check in with your web hosting company, be it GoDaddy or Wix or another. Or, you can explore Google Workspace and see what's involved with adding email to your domain.

If you don't have a domain yet, have some fun picking one. This should be affiliated with your brand name, business, or industry. I use GoDaddy to buy all of my domains.

Date Completed:

Challenge Review

Notes or initial observations:

What worked:

What didn't work:

What will you continue to do?

What will you do differently next time?

DAY 64
CREATE A PROMO VIDEO FOR YOUR SERVICES

Have you ever considered creating a promo video for your business?

A promo video is similar to a TV commercial for your services!

Believe it or not, creating a promo video is easier and less expensive than you think.

Your challenge today is to create a promo video for your Notary business.

The cool thing about this is you don't have to have the technical skills to actually make a video. There's an entire marketplace of highly skilled creatives who can do the technical stuff for you—and they do it relatively inexpensively.

Check out the talented freelancers at Fiverr at https://www.fiverr.com or Upwork at https://www.upwork.com.

Search there for promo video editors or creators and have a conversation with some of the highly rated freelancers. It's okay to be honest with them about your experience level as you share what you'd like to create. They'll get a feel for the scope of the work and quote you a price. Then you decide if it works for you.

Here are a few types of videos to consider:

- **Customer-centric Value Videos**: Check out Jennifer Cooper's video blog series here: https://jkcmobilenotary.com/youtube-videos. Jen records these on her phone, speaking to her ideal customers, delivering value about topics such as home buying, etc. This gives people a chance to get to know, like, and trust her as the expert Notary in her city. She even edits her own videos and includes music and a graphic. Once you learn how to do this on your own, it won't cost you anything but time to create videos like this.

- **Service Reel Videos**: This is an excellent way to start with video, especially if you're a little camera-shy. You can turn PowerPoint slides, screenshots, images, etc., into a video with music. Check out Jeff Clark's home page here for an example of how this might work:

https://www.acmenotary.com. I found a guy on Fiverr who will create videos like this, where he combines videos of me talking with applicable slides from a PowerPoint for just $70 per video, and he's on the higher end of the cost spectrum. He also has hundreds of five-star reviews!

- **Highly Produced Videos**: These videos can be anything you want them to be. You can be talking in front of a prominent building, such as your state capitol. Or, you can splice together stock videos (free or paid portions of videos of other people, places, and things) and have a narrator deliver your message. And that narrator could totally be you, or you can find one on Fiverr too.

Here is an example video we had produced for NBB members who want more escrow direct relationships: https://rfnfo.com/res/29625/130722?source=mobile.

Where can you use your new video?

The options are endless!

You can use these videos in social media or on your website/blog, of course. Or, I am a fan of using them as a way to differentiate yourself after a networking meeting or after you've just met someone. Send them a friendly text with an invitation to watch a video about what makes you special.

Video works!

You'll see.

Date Completed:

Challenge Review

Notes or initial observations:

What worked:

What didn't work:

What will you continue to do?

What will you do differently next time?

DAY 65
MAKE A LIST OF NEW INCOME STREAMS

Are you thinking about diversifying your income streams?

I grew up reading books by Warren Buffet and Robert Kiyosaki (among others) that advocated developing up to seven different revenue streams to bring peace of mind and financial independence.

And a recent mentor of mine is up to 44 streams of income!

On a more micro level, as mobile Notaries and loan signing agents, we need to diversify our services and revenue streams as well. Most of us are feeling the pinch with the drop in refinance transactions, so we need a supplemental stream of income as the market recovers.

Here are some additional revenue stream ideas under the Notary Umbrella:

- Specialty Notary work

- Apostille agent

- Fingerprinting

- Wedding officiant

- Field inspections

- Permit runner

- Process server

What else can you think of?

Your challenge today is to write out a list of the various revenue stream possibilities you'd like to explore and add to your services now or in the future.

Here's another thing I love about this gig: As a credentialed professional with mobility, we can do SO MUCH in a convenience economy.

Some other ideas:

- Technology pro (help others with RON or DocuSign tech)

- Photo verifications

- Surveys

- Signature gathering

- Document presentation

You can also diversify your revenue outside of this business, right?

Here are some popular ways to do so (find links on the Readers Resource Website at www.NotaryCoach.com/90):

- Invest in real estate.

- Rent your cars on Turo (like Airbnb for cars).

- Buy a franchise.

- Invest in a new technology or company.

- Buy an existing company.

- Become an Amazon Business wholesale vendor.

- Open an Etsy shop.

I've done all of these at some point in life, and I love investing in businesses now. My favorite way to get my wheels turning is to scroll through the listings on BizBuySell at https://www.bizbuysell.com. I bought a liquor store on there once. What a blast!

Make your list, explore your options, and take some action.

You don't have to make any decisions today, but you need to begin brainstorming and planning for yourself. Once you plant the seed, watch for the opportunities that seem to suddenly drop in your lap.

Date Completed:

Challenge Review

Notes or initial observations:

What worked:

What didn't work:

What will you continue to do?

What will you do differently next time?

DAY 66
WRITE A LINKEDIN RECOMMENDATION

We've talked quite a bit about reviews in this Notary Funnel Challenge.

Today, we will talk about the close cousin of the review—the recommendation.

What's the difference?

Well, reviews are usually associated with clients or customers giving their opinion about a product, brand, or service. These can be both positive and negative.

A recommendation is usually one professional sharing their experience in working with, or working for, another professional. And a major difference is that a recommendation is always positive. Otherwise it wouldn't be a recommendation.

Your challenge today is to offer a LinkedIn Recommendation to someone you have loved working with or for.

Why LinkedIn?

Well, LinkedIn makes giving a recommendation super easy to do.

Plus, if you're going to give someone a recommendation, you might as well do it somewhere their peers and potential customers might see it. That's the whole idea!

Here's how to do it:

- First, have a conversation with the person you'd like to make a recommendation about. Simply say, "Hey Jon, I would love to write a LinkedIn recommendation for you. In particular, I'd like to share the exceptional levels of customer service I've seen you demonstrate through the years of working with you at ABC Title. Would that be okay with you?"

- Once you get the recipient's buy-in on a recommendation, simply log in to LinkedIn and go to their profile.

- Click on "More" in the top section.

- Choose 'Recommend" from the drop-down menu.

- LinkedIn will then prompt you to fill in three fields: 1) Relationship to the recipient (from drop-down menu), 2) Recipient's position at the time of the great experience you had (from drop-down menu), and 3) Your written recommendation, which can be up to 3,000 characters long.

I recommend being as descriptive as possible and make the recommendation longer than you might for something like a restaurant review. Be specific and speak to the character of the individual as well as to the value they have brought to your life or your audience.

If you really want to go next level with this, make this a habit by writing a recommendation every week (or however often you choose), being sure to add it to your schedule. There is no such thing as giving too many recommendations!

Who can you recommend?

You can write a recommendation for literally anyone with whom you have had an awesome professional experience! Here are a few ideas:

- Escrow officers

- Real estate agents

- Loan officers

- Plumbers

- Coaches

- Mentors

- Authors

- Teachers

- Your employers

- Your managers

- Drivers

- Store or restaurant owners

- Anyone with a LinkedIn profile is a candidate!

Speak from your own experience working with the individual. What have you witnessed? How have they helped you? Why do you love working with them or for them?

Think from a prospective client's perspective. What would a prospective customer want to know about the person they are about to hire? Share your thoughts and help them get hired.

That's the gift of a powerful recommendation!

Date Completed:

Challenge Review

Notes or initial observations:

What worked:

What didn't work:

What will you continue to do?

What will you do differently next time?

DAY 67
KNOW YOUR ENNEAGRAM TYPE

This will be a fun day in the Notary Funnel Challenge.

It's another voyage of self-discovery!

Wheeeeeeeeeee . . .

Knowing yourself, and how you show up to the world, is one of the greatest gifts you bring to your business (and your life). We've talked about a few ways to do that earlier in the NFC, but today I am going to introduce you to the one activity I credit with helping me become a person of purpose.

Your challenge today is to explore the Enneagram and self-identify which type most closely resonates with you.

The Enneagram is a system that defines nine interconnected personality types and is generally used in both business management and spirituality contexts. To determine your Enneagram personality type requires self-assessment.

I highly recommend you use the resources from my own personal business coach, Linda Frazee, on the Readers Resource Website at www.NotaryCoach.com/90. Linda has been teaching the Enneagram and blending it into her business coaching practice for forty years.

On her website, LindaFrazee.com, you'll find a brief overview of the Enneagram, along with a more in-depth description of each of the nine types. To complete today's challenge, simply read through each number and see which one sounds the most like you.

Then, just for kicks, try to figure out which numbers match the people you live with.

Have some fun with it!

Better yet, get into Linda's orbit yourself and join her Authentic Wisdom Community. Linda teaches regular live classes and panel discussions, plus has a whole library of resources.

You can learn more about—and join—Linda's Authentic Wisdom Community here: https://www.lindafrazee.com/authentic-community.

Knowing myself to this depth—strengths, weaknesses, and everything in between—has been a critical factor in my success.

The Enneagram is more popular now than ever. There are countless YouTube channels and websites available for exploration. Even if you choose not to work with Linda directly, find a teacher who resonates with you. And, most uniquely to the Enneagram, be leery of online tests or assessments that promise to tell you what number you are. The Enneagram is about the motivation behind your behavior, and you're the only one who knows that.

Date Completed:

Challenge Review

Notes or initial observations:

What worked:

What didn't work:

What will you continue to do?

What will you do differently next time?

DAY 68
JOIN A LOCAL BAR ASSOCIATION

Have you identified attorneys as your ideal customers?

If so, you'll love today's challenge.

Today, your challenge is to explore the nonlawyer membership and sponsorship opportunities with a local bar association.

A bar association is a professional organization of licensed attorneys across a country. There are many different types and chapters of bar associations on the national, state, and local level. Local bar associations are often county-based, but can also be based in a city or range of suburbs. In addition, specialty bar associations exist at the local level, including those for women and minority lawyers as well as for lawyers practicing in a specific area, such as real estate. Do a Google search for bar associations in your state to find the various options.

In some jurisdictions, association membership is limited to lawyers only. But in others, there may be a nonlawyer membership offered at a significant discount and with some extraordinary benefits, such as these:

- Access to the member database including email addresses

- Invitations to meetings and events

- Opportunity to participate in committees

Regardless of membership rules, many of these organizations have publications and events with opportunities for sponsorships and ads. These could be for you!

Your job as a business owner is to hang out wherever your ideal customers hang out.

If you have decided you want to work with attorneys, start hanging out with attorneys.

A bar association is an excellent place to start.

Date Completed:

Challenge Review

Notes or initial observations:

What worked:

What didn't work:

What will you continue to do?

What will you do differently next time?

DAY 69
CONNECT WITH SOMEONE NEW ON LINKEDIN

What if there was one place online where most of your ideal customers hang out?

Well, that place for most of us as mobile Notaries and loan signing agents is LinkedIn.

Why LinkedIn?

- LinkedIn has more than 850 million users worldwide.

- Many of those users are decision makers in industries that utilize Notaries a lot (real estate, medical, legal).

- LinkedIn is considered the most trusted social media platform.

- 73% of buyers are more likely to consider a brand or service if contact is made on LinkedIn.

Your challenge today is to simply connect with someone new on LinkedIn—with a connection message.

That second part is important. Connect with a message, not simply a blind connect request. People you don't know, especially senior-level executives and true professionals, will want to understand why you are trying to connect with them. If it's someone who is already an acquaintance, remind them how you know them or deepen the connection with a personalized note.

Whom to connect with

You can scroll through some of your phone contacts and hunt for them on LinkedIn.

Or, you can simply watch your LinkedIn feed and see what pops up. You'll see some of the activity of your current connections. Are they liking, commenting on, or sharing a post by someone you might like to get to know?

When you're logged in, LinkedIn also offers you suggestions to connect with "People you may know." You'll often see these suggestions in the column to the right of a profile you're currently viewing.

I also like to connect to authors whose books I have read and enjoy.

What to say

First rule when you send your first message: Do NOT sell anything.

Simply be yourself and tell them why you'd like to connect..

Keep your message short, sweet, and personally related to them.

Here's an example:

"Hi John—A colleague of mine shared an article you wrote on LinkedIn, and I can tell you're passionate about helping seniors navigate retirement. This is a sector I too am passionate about, and I'd love to connect here on LinkedIn. Maybe we can even meet to discuss what a good referral might be for you. Thanks for your time!"

Use today's challenge to practice connecting.

Then keep going!

NBB Resource: *NBB members receive guidance from one of the world's foremost LinkedIn trainers, Sandra Long. She's written the book on it, literally! Plus, she delivered the first TEDx Talk about LinkedIn and how to cultivate relationships on the platform. In NBB, she teaches a monthly class and offers access to her prestigious video course, "LinkedIn Professional Profile."*

Join NBB here for access: https://www.notarycoach.com/nbbfresh.

Date Completed:

Challenge Review

Notes or initial observations:

What worked:

What didn't work:

What will you continue to do?

What will you do differently next time?

DAY 70
YOUR DAILY GURU

As we grow our business, mastering our mindset is crucial.

We aren't necessarily born with these skills. We have to learn them and hone them. And to do so, you should expose yourself to new teachers.

As I was pulling myself out of the depths of depression and failure when my businesses failed, I included a daily practice of five to fifteen minutes to simply watch or listen to teachers of different skills, philosophies, and ways of thinking.

I called this my "Daily Guru."

I simply found someone who either had achieved the results I wanted or demonstrated a behavior or way of being I wanted to learn more about. Then, I added them to my daily calendar. Depending on who it is, and what platforms they teach from, I'll block this time to listen to a speech or podcast, watch a video or training module, or simply read something they've written.

Your challenge today is to identify your own Daily Gurus you'd like to learn more about.

Here are a few of my gurus, both from the past and some new ones, and the topics that originally drew me to them:

- Jack Canfield—Self-Confidence
- Oprah Winfrey—Overcoming obstacles
- Brené Brown—Vulnerability
- Brendan Burchard—Building an online course and collaboration
- Eckhart Tolle—Living in the present moment
- Hal Elrod—Self-confidence and daily success routine
- Chandler Bolt—Self-publishing a book and scaling a business
- Michael Hyatt—Implementing goals with a plan
- Bob Proctor—Abundant thinking

- Mary Morrisey—Thinking bigger and creating a vision

- Linda Frazee—Applying the Enneagram to life

- Robert Kiyosaki—Basics of money and investing

- Tony Robbins—Advanced money understanding

- Ray Edwards—Copywriting strategies

I learned much more than I expected from every one of them, and even eventually built relationships with a few of them, too.

Your own topics and interests may very well differ from mine. That's as it should be!

Choose topics—and people—that you're genuinely interested in. This is you taking responsibility for your own education. You can learn whatever it is you believe will help you be a better businessperson or a better human being.

I recommend scheduling these appointments with your Daily Gurus in advance, as part of your Sunday Success Ritual. Maybe Mondays are for Mary Morrisey. And Wednesdays are for Laura Biewer. See, you can absolutely include your business gurus too!

Date Completed:

Challenge Review

Notes or initial observations:

What worked:

What didn't work:

What will you continue to do?

What will you do differently next time?

DAY 71
ATTEND A TOASTMASTERS MEETING

Toastmasters changed my life.

If you've never heard of them, as they put it, "Toastmasters International is a world leader in communication and leadership development."

They are often thought of as a public-speaking organization. And they are, but they're much more than that.

When I was in full hustle mode as a loan signing agent, it was often difficult for me to find a networking meeting that I could commit to attending every week. My schedule always changed, sometimes minute to minute, so I often petered out on groups that met midday or evenings.

So I started looking for morning meetings. Early morning meetings.

And I found a Toastmasters group that started at 6:00 a.m. every Thursday.

I had heard that Toastmasters could help with public speaking, but frankly, I didn't want to be a public speaker. But I did want to be around people who were on fire with their dreams.

And that's exactly what I found in the Toastmasters meetings. These were people with something to say—and they wanted to help people. They wanted to change the world.

My kind of networking.

The "side effect" of attending these meetings, and eventually taking on roles and speaking, was that I learned how to present information better. And what do we do all day as an LSA? We present documents all day. Toastmasters is where my document scripts and appointment organization were born.

This also is what helped give me the confidence to finally get on YouTube, where likely you and I were connected.

Then came my course. Then my first book. Then speaking gigs.

Toastmasters welcomes guests, and usually for free. Sure, they have membership options. But find your people first. Find a group that makes you feel warm, welcome, and safe. Even if it's a bit uncomfortable at first. Growth comes through discomfort.

Today your challenge is to find a Toastmasters meeting near you and schedule your attendance.

Learn more about Toastmasters here:

https://www.toastmasters.org/about/all-about-toastmasters.

And here's something super cool: My friend Dan Brewer, himself a Distinguished Toastmaster, organizes a Notary Toastmasters group called "Notary Masters." This is an online and nationwide group just for Notaries to hone their skills and connect.

Check out Notary Masters here: https://notarymasters.org/.

Whether you want to connect with your fellow Notaries through Notary Masters or with your ideal customers through a more general Toastmasters group, you'll find friends and colleagues who will lift you up when you need it most.

That's what high performers do when they're out changing the world—they lift up those around them.

> "The ones who are crazy enough to think they can change the world are the ones who do."
>
> —Steve Jobs

Date Completed:

Challenge Review

Notes or initial observations:

What worked:

What didn't work:

What will you continue to do?

What will you do differently next time?

DAY 72
SEND A THANK-YOU TO
SOMEONE WHO HELPED

The more you incorporate gratitude into your business, the more you're going to love it.

Today, your challenge is to write a thank-you note to someone who has helped you along the way.

This person can be anyone of your choosing, from any time period of your life:

- Your father-in-law, who loaned you money to buy your first house

- That friend who helped you work on your car

- The mentor who spent extra time with you

- Your mom, who went above and beyond

- The client who fed you after hearing your tummy growl at an appointment (been there!)

You're surrounded by people who love and support you.

Let's send them a handwritten card to acknowledge it.

These notes don't have to be the length of a novel. They can be short and sweet. A little vulnerability can open doors, too.

"Hey Frank,

I was thinking about you the other day. When you helped Carla and me buy our house, it helped give us the foundation we needed to start our family and build a life together. I want you to know how grateful I am for that generous act of kindness. Thank you!

Bob

PS See you Sunday for dinner? We've got cornhole set up in the backyard and the kids will be here."

Have some fun with it. Get creative. Be yourself.

Date Completed:

Challenge Review

Notes or initial observations:

What worked:

What didn't work:

What will you continue to do?

What will you do differently next time?

DAY 73
DECIDE WHETHER TO BECOME
AN APOSTILLE AGENT

Until a couple years ago, most of us had no idea what an apostille agent was.

These days, the apostille opportunity is a mainstream conversation in our industry.

Why is that?

I have a few theories.

First, my friend and colleague Judi Lawrence blazed a trail with training and resources about the opportunity.

And then Judi and Matt Miller wrote a book about it.

Now there are several other trainers across the country teaching the ins and outs of being an apostille agent.

Then interest rates went up.

So Notaries are looking for additional ways to earn money.

And being an apostille agent can be lucrative.

Open to all fifty states (yep, yours too) and Washington, DC.

Your challenge today is to dive in and decide if you want to add apostille agent to your toolbox.

Yay or nay, the choice is yours. Just make the choice. Don't let it linger in your brain, taking up space: "I should look at that apostille thing."

No more "shoulding" on yourself.

Make the call. Yes or no.

If no, keep your eye out for something else—the right opportunity for you.

If yes, join us in NBB and get access to Judi's six-week master class here: https://www.notarycoach.com/nbbfresh.

Or, if you'd rather access Judi's training directly from her, you can register for her class at a discount using the link on the Readers Resource Website at www.NotaryCoach.com/90.

And you can order Judi and Matt's *Apostille Agents' Survival Guide* here: https://allaboutapostilles.com/. If you get the Kindle edition, you can start reading within seconds.

Date Completed:

Challenge Review

Notes or initial observations:

What worked:

What didn't work:

What will you continue to do?

What will you do differently next time?

DAY 74
CHECK YOUR WEBSITE'S GOOGLE PAGE RANK

Are you ready to have your mind blown?

Sometimes our own website pages can be interfering with our Google ranking!

It's hard enough to boost our website's page rank in our city, and without a little review and attention, sometimes we could be jamming it up.

I'll show you what I mean.

- Bring up your website on a computer or laptop (way easier than using your phone for this).

- Then, in the front of the URL (e.g., https://www.YOUR WEBSITE.com), type the word **site:** (including the colon and with no spaces after it). The resulting URL should be in this format— **site:https://www.YOURWEBSITE.com**

- Press Enter and you'll be taken to a Google search page. These are all the pages of YOUR website that Google recognizes. In other words, Google knows these pages exist with content and is "crawling" these pages. Take a look around. Are any of your pages missing? Is Google blind to your most important pages, like your Services page? If all your pages are there, how does Google rank them in authority and relevance?

- Then, check this out. Scroll back up to the Google search bar at the top of the page. Likely, site:https://www.YOURWEBSITE.com is still populated there, and that's a good thing. Leave that language in the search box and hit the spacebar at the end. Type a keyword or phrase that you have been working to rank for. You might try words such as "Notary near me," or "Santa Cruz Mobile Notary," or "Jacksonville Wedding Officiant," or "Santa Fe Apostille."

The results you'll see are how Google has ranked the pages of YOUR website in relevance and authority to the keywords you just added.

How does it look to you?

What page is ranked at the top when you're using "[Your city name] Notary Public"?

Is it your Services page?

Is it the page you want potential customers to land on? You know, the one with a clear call to action and your phone number or automated scheduling system?

Or, is it your Blog page, or your About page, where it might be harder to find your contact info or details on the services you provide?

These small technical details can actually be a HUGE obstacle on your road to converting prospects who happen to find your website into customers that actually pay for your services.

It's almost as though our own website is cannibalizing our own page's Google rankings.

To combat this, use some of that content from the other pages and add it to the key page you want to rank higher. You can even use a redirect (or forward) to send those who click the higher-ranked page to the actual sales page or services page you want them to land on.

Ranking is awesome.

Ranking for the right words and content is better.

Combining those two so that customers find what they need and you get new clients is the trifecta.

Date Completed:

Challenge Review

Notes or initial observations:

What worked:

What didn't work:

What will you continue to do?

What will you do differently next time?

DAY 75
TITLE YOUR VIDEOS FOR MAXIMUM VIEWS

Are you making videos yet?

I know it's uncomfortable, but they sure are powerful ways for customers to get to know you, like you, and trust you.

If you're already making videos to help attract your ideal customers, you'll appreciate today's challenge.

Today, you'll title your videos using keywords that drive maximum views.

Google is the biggest search engine in the world. The second largest? YouTube.

And guess who owns YouTube . . . Google!

Google loves Google.

And the world pretty much knows that you can learn just about anything you need to know on YouTube. So your videos need to be there, AND with great titles that help your content rank for views and value.

Here are a few tips for titling videos:

- Research the exact keywords and phrases your ideal customers are using to find the answers or services they need, and USE these keywords and phrases toward the beginning of your video titles.

- If possible, keep titles under 70 characters to avoid truncation.

- If you're looking for hyper-local traffic in your city, as we often do as mobile Notaries and loan signing agents, don't be afraid to use your geographic area in the titles.

Here are some examples:

- "3 Ways to Prepare for a Notary Appointment in Chicago"

- "How to Save Money on Your Apostille in Florida"

- "Ohio Real ID Requirements Change Abruptly"

- "How a Top-Performing L.A. Lawyer Doubles Revenue by Using a Notary"

Have some fun with this and keep making great content!

Date Completed:

Challenge Review

Notes or initial observations:

What worked:

What didn't work:

What will you continue to do?

What will you do differently next time?

DAY 76
BRAINSTORM TOPICS FOR VIDEOS
YOU COULD MAKE

Since we talked about titling videos yesterday, I thought I might continue the conversation today.

It can be truly intimidating to learn how to create videos, but boy do they work!

Rest assured you don't need a bunch of technical equipment to get started. In fact, you can use your phone to make most videos.

And whether you're just getting started or you've already been pumping out some content, knowing what to talk about next is a constant challenge.

So today's challenge is to brainstorm topics for the different videos you could make.

Let me start you off with a few ideas:

- Recommend a book your ideal customers should be reading right now.

- Share the story of the first customer you ever helped.

- Explain how your morning routine sets you up for success.

- Reveal the biggest misconception about what you do as a Notary.

- Share a personal story of the family struggle when someone dies intestate.

- Provide a tip your ideal customer could implement right now to make life easier or bring them closer to a goal.

There are so many ways you can go with a video!

Let your personality shine through and stay committed to delivering value by helping people.

Date Completed:

Challenge Review

Notes or initial observations:

What worked:

What didn't work:

What will you continue to do?

What will you do differently next time?

DAY 77
CREATE AN OUTLINE FOR YOUR VIDEOS

I promise this will be the final challenge involving videos.

Can you tell they're important?

Today's challenge is to create an outline for your next video (and then use it as a template for future videos).

So, maybe you bought in on videos yesterday and created a list of ten you could create over the next few months.

What now, right?

Well, let me give you a quick outline that can help guide your video conversation.

First, come up with a way you'd like to start each video. Don't worry, this can change over the lifespan of your business, but when you begin each video in about the same way it actually helps you kick off the presentation without stumbling over words as much. (Don't get me wrong; you're going to stumble, and that is TOTALLY okay! That's what editing is for.)

Here's one idea: "Hi everyone, this is your Notary Ninja Nicky serving up integrity, courtesy, and knowledge in Atlanta, Georgia, and today I'm talking about . . ."

Have one big concept or idea in mind for each video (using the ideas you came up with yesterday).

Spark interest with an opening line—something to get people interested in what you're about to share, often called a "hook." Maybe something like, "Hey estate planning attorneys, did you know you can earn more money without leaving the beach? In today's video I share . . ."

Then, deliver the goods. What are three or four solid points you want to leave with the viewer?

Finally, what action do you want people to take after watching? Again, this is called the call to action or CTA. And with clarity on this, you'll win more customers. A solid CTA could be anything from "Subscribe to my Channel" to "Click the link below to book a consultation" to simply "Buy here."

So here is what your video outline looks like:

- Scripted intro for all or most videos

- Overarching theme or topic for video

- Opening hook

- Point #1

- Point #2

- Point #3

- Call to Action

You can create your own video outline in Word, or use something fancier. You are the only one who needs to see it.

Date Completed:

Challenge Review

Notes or initial observations:

What worked:

What didn't work:

What will you continue to do?

What will you do differently next time?

DAY 78
BEST DIRECTORIES FOR FINDING ATTORNEYS

Are attorneys part of your ideal customer base?

The legal industry uses Notaries even more than the mortgage industry.

Whichever niche you've identified as bringing more joy or revenue into your business, I have some excellent resources that can help you find attorneys to connect with.

Your challenge today is to simply peruse attorney directories to find a few lawyers in your area who look like prospects to you.

You may be surprised by how many attorneys are located near you.

As I am building out my own business, working with estate planning attorneys, I am learning that their start-up and hustle is very similar to ours. They often work as solo-preneurs, wearing all the hats and doing all the things, in order to build their dreams.

You can help them.

Here are five attorney directories you can use to build a hot prospect list:

- AVVO: https://www.avvo.com/

- FindLaw: https://www.findlaw.com/

- Lawyers.com: https://www.lawyers.com/

- Abogado (Spanish-speaking lawyers): https://www.abogado.com/directorio.html

- The Bar Association Directory: https://www.barassociationdirectory.com/

You can also find these links on the Readers Resource Website at www.NotaryCoach.com/90.

Have fun exploring and helping!

Date Completed:

Challenge Review

Notes or initial observations:

What worked:

What didn't work:

What will you continue to do?

What will you do differently next time?

DAY 79
GET A DIGITAL BUSINESS CARD

Have you ever seen a digital business card?

These are actually pretty cool and all the rage right now.

Check out my digital business card here:
https://rfnfo.com/dc/259/130722?source=web

This comes in handy for use in my email signatures, or when I meet someone and want to get all my info to them in one QUICK step.

When we tell people we're a Notary, many want our info right away.

Business cards are great and, as we discussed back on Day 13, they continue to be important. But in a digitized world, it serves you to play there too.

Look how easy it is for the recipient of my digital business card to save all my contact information to their phone or computer with the click of a button.

Impressive, right?

Your challenge today is to find a digital business card solution that fits your budget.

Choose something that is easy to use, too. All the cool tech tools in the world mean nothing if you don't use them.

Save the info from my digital card and keep it handy as well. Let me know how I can support you along the way.

NBB Resource: *As part of Notary Business Builder, we offer a complimentary digital business card (like mine) in our TOMM app. It's yours when you join at www.NotaryCoach.com/nbbfresh.*

Date Completed:

Challenge Review

Notes or initial observations:

What worked:

What didn't work:

What will you continue to do?

What will you do differently next time?

DAY 80
RECORD A PROFESSIONAL
VOICEMAIL GREETING

Let's go back to basics for a minute.

We wear so many freakin' hats as mobile Notaries, things sometimes slip through the cracks.

This isn't always a big deal, of course. But every now and again, these little things might actually impact our business.

Things like having a professional voicemail greeting is an example of that.

Your first impression matters to prospects. It's easy to justify letting it slide or de-prioritizing it because no one ever mentions it.

But guess what: What people *don't* say can actually be what kills your business. Because they can make the decision to hire a different Notary and you'll never know it. This is an easy fix. We can't control everything, but our voicemail greeting is 100% under our control.

Your challenge today is to record a professional email greeting for your business line.

Don't rely on the standard recorded messages like "You have reached 555-555-5555, please leave a message after the tone." Similarly, don't record messages like, "Yo, it's me. Leave a message at the beep."

You're in business. Time for your voicemail greeting to reflect that.

Here are some ideas:

- Use a warm, friendly, and even enthusiastic tone of voice. Are you a professional? Do you want more business? Show it!

- Keep it informative and upbeat. "Hi, you've reached Tanya at Mobile Notary Experts of Nashville. I am likely with a client right now, but can *usually* call you back within an hour. Or if you text me at the same number, I may be able to respond faster. Thank you; I look forward to being of service!"

- If you want to go a little further, record a new message every day with the date so people know you're on duty and ready to serve.

Date Completed:

Challenge Review

Notes or initial observations:

What worked:

What didn't work:

What will you continue to do?

What will you do differently next time?

DAY 81
HOW TO "CLOSE THE SALE"
ON GNW/SNW CALLS

You're working hard to bring more customers into your business.

So what happens when your hard work starts paying off and your phone starts ringing and dinging with more general notary work (GNW) and specialty notary work (SNW) calls?

Getting the phone to ring is only one part of it. Closing the sale or setting the appointment is a whole other thing.

And make no mistake about it—these Notary service calls that come in ARE sales calls.

You're not in the answering service business. You're a Notary practitioner. That means if you ain't notarizing, you ain't gettin' paid.

So how do you convert more of your calls into actual paid appointments?

Here's the framework for a call flow that works:

- Answer the phone.

- Have a plan in place to communicate or set expectations when you can't answer the phone.

- Answer and communicate with warm, friendly tones and vocabulary.

- Politely overcome the first question most people ask first: "How much is it to get this notarized?"

- Demonstrate your expertise and ask probing questions.

- Repeat back everything involved as you understand it.

- Quote the scope of the assignment with the price estimate.

- Seal the deal: "If that sounds good to you, Mr. Bradbury, I can be at your home on Warner Street at 7:00 p.m. this evening, as requested."

Your challenge today is to examine this call flow framework and adopt the pieces that could convert more appointments for you.

You don't have to love every piece of this. What works for me and hundreds of others may not work for you, and that's okay.

Tweak it. Make it your own.

How will you know it works?

Results.

Results don't lie.

Keep refining your processes. You've worked hard for this. Every time that phone rings, you have an opportunity to expertly deliver your services and win a customer for life.

The process deserves your attention.

Date Completed:

Challenge Review

Notes or initial observations:

What worked:

What didn't work:

What will you continue to do?

What will you do differently next time?

DAY 82
ADD A NEW PHOTO TO YOUR
GOOGLE BUSINESS PROFILE

I know you've been listening, right?

So you have already completed your Google Business Profile.

Want more customers? Got to have it!

Today your challenge is to take a photo and add it to your Google Business Profile.

Yeah, this challenge is a simple one. And, it's an important one, especially if you turn this into a habit!

Google is smart, but it needs your help.

Posting photos can legitimize your business in the "eyes" of Google. It lets them know that you're active. And, if you post fresh content with that photo, it lets Google know if you're relevant to their customers' online searches.

Most importantly, when you take the photo using an iPhone or Android with Location Services turned on, the photos will have metadata that reflect the geographic location. This is extremely helpful in hyper-local marketing!

Take photos of yourself at work, a favorite coffee house, area attractions, shops, mountains—whatever is interesting and brings you joy or establishes your passion and expertise.

If you happen to have a physical location that customers can come to, this is even more important. With your Location Services turned on, take at least twenty interior photos and twenty exterior photos of your location and post them in the applicable areas of your Google Business Profile. And, if you have multiple locations, have a separate Google Business Profile for every location. Repeat the photo strategy for each as well.

Date Completed:

Challenge Review

Notes or initial observations:

What worked:

What didn't work:

What will you continue to do?

What will you do differently next time?

DAY 83
IMPLEMENT PSA MARKETING STRATEGY

I think one of the reasons you and I are here together is that we like to help people.

In today's challenge we get to ramp that up even more.

I know I teased and said I wouldn't talk about videos again, but this challenge works and I think you'll love it.

This is known as the PSA approach:

1. Pick a topic that you've had some experience with, either directly or through a friend, family, or client (keep all personal info out of these; it's not needed for impact).

2. Make a video that simply informs people about the issue, the law change, the misunderstanding—whatever it is.

3. Give them resources for solutions without ever selling your services. You can say things like, "Check with your favorite Notary for more information" or with whoever may be the best resource. This is strictly a Public Service Announcement.

The best use for this is on your own social media pages, such as Instagram, Facebook, Twitter, and even LinkedIn. If you leave out the "selling" part and keep this 100% PSA, your friends and family (and all followers) are more likely to share the video to their own pages and feeds.

This magnifies the potential audience for your video by over a hundredfold and allows people you'd never have talked to before to get to know you, like you, and trust you because you're sharing valuable information.

Your challenge today is to implement the three-step PSA approach.

Think about your topic. What have you witnessed or what has happened to you? Ever been a victim of identity theft? Ever have a loved one die without a will or trust? Ever have a car overheat on the freeway? You could go all kinds of directions with this.

Earlier in the challenge, I gave you an outline for your videos. Use that to highlight your topic, the three or four points you want to make, and a call to action directed to resources that could help. (Remember, do NOT sell yourself here; very few people will share it if you do.)

And, you can even expand beyond Notary resources on these videos. You could talk about things that require an attorney. Or a mechanic. Or a real estate agent. Or a lender.

These PSA videos could be bullhorns for supporting your network. That's an amazing way to be a resource. Think big!

Challenge Review

Notes or initial observations:

What worked:

What didn't work:

What will you continue to do?

What will you do differently next time?

DAY 84
ASK FOR A CHARACTER REVIEW

When you're first starting out and building your online presence with Google Business Profile, a website, LinkedIn, and even Yelp, getting your first few reviews can feel impossible.

First, you may have to overcome some fear or anxiety to even ask for a review in the first place.

Then, when you muster the courage to ask, you have to make it easy for the customer to post the review.

And, even when the customer says yes (as they usually do), sometimes they don't follow through as fast as we'd like them to (or at all).

It can feel like your first reviews take forever to receive!!!

But when they do start coming in, it seems to create a snowball effect. And if you keep asking for reviews, they keep coming.

Here's a strategy to help spark that momentum even faster—leverage the power of a character review.

We were all somebody before we were Notaries. Someone has witnessed us navigate this crazy world we live in, or watched us shine at work in some capacity. There are people in your world who can testify to your integrity, your customer service commitment, your passion, humor, and confidence—your character.

Your challenge today is to ask someone you trust to provide a character review.

Remember to make it easy for them to do this. Here's how the conversation might go:

You: Hey Sue! I am building my new business and I am asking a few people who have seen me work at my best for a character review. If I send you a link, would you be willing to write something in the next few days?

Sue: Sure! Can't wait to hear about the business!

You: Thank you so much! Here is the link to where you can leave the review: www.ReviewsforBob.com (or whatever URL you created to go to your Google Business Profile). Sue, character reviews are more general in scope, so they don't have to be specific about my current business. I'm establishing myself as a leader in my field, so if you could speak to the reasons you promoted me to the supervisor role and our dynamic after the fact, it would be so helpful. Thank you! And I'll text you next week to set a time to catch up. Would be great to see you!

You can have the conversation via text, email, phone, or in person.

There are people in your personal network who think you are amazing. No, they *know* you are amazing. Those are the people you want to ask for these character reviews.

Consider asking people in roles like these, past and present:

- Bosses or managers

- Coworkers

- Business partners

- Life partners

- Longtime friends

- Colleagues

- Mentors

- Coaches

Spark the momentum and then keep it going by sharing your amazingness with your customers and colleagues.

Date Completed:

Challenge Review

Notes or initial observations:

What worked:

What didn't work:

What will you continue to do?

What will you do differently next time?

DAY 85
JOIN ALIGNABLE

It can be difficult to differentiate between scammy stuff and the real deal when you're in business.

It seems as though everyone wants to sell you the next "must have" directory listing, networking group, or doohickie-thingamabopper.

One of the perks I have as a nationwide Notary Coach is to hear what works and what doesn't from top-performing solo-preneurs. And I am hearing some pretty powerful stories about Alignable: The Small Business Referral Network.

Your challenge is to sign up (for free) with Alignable.

I admit, I had ignored the dozens of invites I got to join Alignable every month. I thought it was just another fluff directory that overpromises and underdelivers.

I was wrong!

Alignable is responsible for connections and relationships between Notaries and other professionals, including

- Attorneys

- Real estate agents

- Loan officers

- Escrow officers

- and More!

Sign up for Alignable here: https://www.alignable.com/.

(This link is also available on the Readers Resource Website at www.NotaryCoach.com/90.)

As with all of your directory listings, take the time to fill out your Alignable listing completely and optimize it with your photo, personality, passion, and professionalism. You can't get a feel for the power of a directory if your listing isn't engaging to the people who use the directory.

The stories that are emerging from this network are nothing short of remarkable. Check it out for yourself!

Challenge Review

Notes or initial observations:

What worked:

What didn't work:

What will you continue to do?

What will you do differently next time?

DAY 86
RESPOND TO THREE IMPORTANT QUESTIONS FOR NOTARIES

We're talking about unusual situations in the Notary life today.

Today's challenge is to use your state-specific resources to answer these three questions:

1. Can I certify representative capacity? And if so, do I need to see proof of that capacity?

2. Is signature by proxy allowed in notarized documents in my state? And if so, what are the rules surrounding it?

3. What responsibilities do my heirs have when I die as a Notary Public?

The correct responses to all three of these will be specific to your state. Some handbooks may offer details, while others might be vague. Remember your Hierarchy of Support from the Day 8 Challenge. Where do you go for the answers you need?

Be the MacGyver Notary.

This will help you be a better Notary, and when you know the answers to some of these questions that linger in the mind for a while, it can boost your confidence. You know you've got this, whatever "this" may be.

And particular to question number 3 above . . .

In keeping with the integrity of our office we are obliged to help our heirs follow through with the final responsibilities of a Notary Public. Make sure you let them know what is required of them, whether in your Last Will and Testament or your Trust, or by simply leaving a copy of instructions on what to do should you pass away while in office. Trust me, they won't even be thinking about your journals and stamps. You'll need to guide them.

I've recently partnered with a company that provides a secure online vault for just this purpose. It stores everything your family will need to help make the transition without you less stressful. And you can even provide the instructions and links to rules about what they should do with your old journals and stamps. Check out the Legacy Vault on the Reader's Resource Website at www.NotaryCoach.com/90.

Date Completed:

Challenge Review

Notes or initial observations:

What worked:

What didn't work:

What will you continue to do?

What will you do differently next time?

DAY 87
VISIT A NEW NETWORKING GROUP

We are surrounded by opportunity.

The secret is to connect with people who see the value of your services.

Your challenge today is to visit a new networking group.

You can visit as a guest, and usually for free.

To find a networking group, try these:

- MeetUp: https://www.meetup.com/

- Facebook Events

- Business Networking International

- Toastmasters (an excellent way to train and network)

- Rotary International

- Small Business Administration

- LinkedIn Events and Groups

You are under no obligation to stay or become a member. Remember that.

I didn't enjoy networking events until I gave myself permission to only attend those that made me feel good. The members at those events were warm and gracious. They made me feel welcome. And I felt like I could bring value to them as well.

That's part of being able to show up authentically, and it's incredibly important. You have to feel good when you go to these things, otherwise you won't do it.

Networking does not have to be a sacrifice of your soul. You can be you, enjoy it, and help people.

Find your people!

Date Completed:

Challenge Review

Notes or initial observations:

What worked:

What didn't work:

What will you continue to do?

What will you do differently next time?

DAY 88
DOUBLE-CHECK YOUR NAP

The Google search engine is pretty smart, but it's not perfect.

Sometimes the smallest difference in the way your name, address, or phone number is typed can really jam things up.

Algorithms are finicky.

There's not a little person in there deciding that 123 Broad Street is the same as 123 Broadstreet, or that 555-555-5555 is the same as 555.555.5555, or that William Soroka and Bill Soroka are the same person. To a human that all makes logical sense.

To a computer?

Not so much.

And this can actually negatively impact your search rankings. Why work so hard to ramp up your SEO only to have it sabotaged by these tiny little discrepancies?

Your challenge today is to double-check your NAP—Name | Address | Phone Number—on your digital profiles and website.

What you are looking for across the board is consistency.

If my business, name, address, and phone number is typed out like this once—

Magic Pen Mobile Notary, LLC
William Soroka
123 Broadstreet
Lexington, KY 40502
(555) 555-5555

—then it needs to appear exactly like that everywhere else online.

Every comma. Every abbreviation. Every parenthesis.

Will you still get search engine rankings without going through the process of checking and making all your listings consistent? Absolutely (depending on your competitors' ability to optimize and your market city).

Will you likely miss out on business if you don't do this? Most definitely.

This is part of your refinement process. You have the profiles and directory listings. Now you optimize.

NotaryAssist, the leader in accounting and bookkeeping software for Notaries, now offers an additional service that helps with this. Their Marketing package includes access to a proprietary program that will help you manage your NAP, hours of operation, and more, plus distribute your data to hundreds of online locations. All managed with a few clicks and tons of support!

Explore NotaryAssist Marketing on the Readers Resource Website at www.NotaryCoach.com/90.

Date Completed:

Challenge Review

Notes or initial observations:

What worked:

What didn't work:

What will you continue to do?

What will you do differently next time?

DAY 89
OUTSOURCE A
TIME- (OR JOY-) CONSUMING TASK

Don't let your "but" destroy your dream.

We all have a "but" (or several):

- I want this business to work, BUT I am too intimidated by technology to create a Google Business Profile.

- I want to work hard enough to be successful, BUT someone has to take the time to cook dinner every night.

- I want to focus on making $100,000 per year, BUT laundry doesn't do itself.

- I want my schedule to be my own, BUT if I don't mow the lawn, nobody does.

Yes, technology is key to your business. And people gotta eat. Laundry needs to be clean. Lawns must be kept up. All real.

Done by you and you alone? Not necessarily.

Sometimes we take on more than we need to because it's just the way things have always been done. Or we're afraid to ask for help for one reason or another.

Through years of coaching Notaries and other small business owners, I've heard all the "buts." I've also seen overwhelming evidence that you are likely surrounded by people who love you and want to support you; they just don't know how yet. Hard truth—it's your responsibility to ask for support, or make known how to support you, not theirs to psychically know.

Enroll them in the dream and get the support you crave.

So, what's the "but" in the way of *your* dream right now?

Your challenge today is to identify and outsource something that sucks the joy or energy out of your life right now.

Building a business isn't easy. It's exhausting. You need every ounce of energy you have.

Every time a "but" gets in the way, stop and take a look at it. Who can help?

Outsourcing doesn't necessarily mean you have to pay someone else to do something.

Recruit family.

Trade services.

Or go ahead and hire a service; the return on your investment will be worth it.

Your dream and those you are building it for, including yourself, will thank you later.

My productivity surged when I hired a housekeeper and a landscaper. I was no longer distracted by activities I dreaded anyway, and I could focus on building my business, or . . . having fun!

Isn't that what we work for when we boil it down? To do more things we love with the people we love.

Date Completed:

Challenge Review

Notes or initial observations:

What worked:

What didn't work:

What will you continue to do?

What will you do differently next time?

DAY 90
DISCOVER THE LINKEDIN QR CODE

There's a supercharged way to connect at networking or professional events.

I think this is a brilliant LinkedIn feature.

Using the LinkedIn app on your smartphone, you can quickly connect with people using a special QR code. These codes are scannable, so the person you are meeting can simply hover their phone's camera over the QR code and your LinkedIn profile will immediately populate on their screen and you two can connect.

Your challenge today is to discover your LinkedIn QR code and use it at your next event to connect to someone new.

Here's how to find it:

- Open the LinkedIn app on your mobile phone.

- Tap into the Search box.

- At the far right of the search box, you'll see a square graphic—that's the QR code symbol. Tap it.

- On the screen that comes up, under the "My code" tab, you'll see a box with your name and title above a QR Code—this is your personalized QR Code. A jumble of a design that technology somehow can read.

Cool, right?

The person you are meeting just points their phone's camera lens at it and a link will pop up for them to tap. That link will be your LinkedIn profile so they can connect to you, assuming they are also on LinkedIn.

You can do the same if they have a QR code too.

To make it even easier, you can also save your code to your image gallery.

Almost everyone that you may consider an ideal customer is on LinkedIn.

Impress them with your skills and your knowledge.

Sometimes finding the QR code on your phone will vary on your device. There is a link to LinkedIn's instructions for this on the Readers Resource Website at www.NotaryCoach.com/90.

Be sure we are connected on LinkedIn as well. You can follow me or connect with a message here: https://www.linkedin.com/in/billsoroka/.

Date Completed:

Challenge Review

Notes or initial observations:

What worked:

What didn't work:

What will you continue to do?

What will you do differently next time?

RINSE & REPEAT

Congratulations! You've completed the initial 90 days of the Notary Business Builder Challenge.

By implementing these strategies, you'll bring more peace of mind to yourself and land more clients.

But you still have more work to do. There's always room for refinement, new ideas, and new skills. You can use this book as a guide throughout the year.

With approximately 90 days in each fiscal quarter, you could refer to this book every single day of the year and adjust the exercises within to your particular needs.

A powerful benefit of reading—and learning in general—is how it can spark dynamic ideas of your own. There's no one single road to success—there are millions. My perspective and experience are just that, mine. You have your own as well, and you're every bit as worthy of success.

Take this material and make it your own. Build a business that you love and enjoy. And honor it for what it can be to your customers. The rest will inevitably fall into place.

Find Free Resources and Tools on the
Readers Resource Website at:

www.NotaryCoach.com/90

ACKNOWLEDGMENTS

This book would not have been possible without there first being a place for graduate-level Notaries and mentors to congregate and share information. It is with enormous gratitude that I thank the following people for having the trust, faith, and wisdom, to invest their precious resources into the Notary Business Builder Advanced Notary Mastermind.

Notary Business Builder is an elite community of advanced Notary entrepreneurs who are committed to building a successful business in *any* economy by leveraging authentic sharing technology and cultivating deeper relationships. In order to make a vision of that scale a reality, it was necessary to collaborate with sages from multiple specialites. This is how NBB became a one-stop shop for everything you need to succeed in this business—the people, the courses, and the technology.

Special thanks to the following people for making Notary Business Builder—and this 90-Day Challenge book—a reality:

Laura Biewer, founder of CoachMeLaura.com and creator of the annual Notary Symposium;

Jennifer Neitzel, founder of Signing Agent Marketing (SAM);

Judi Lawrence, founder of the Lawrence Institute for Notaries and the World of Apostille Masterclass;

Sandra Long, author of *LinkedIn for Personal Branding* and co-author of *Supercharge Your Notary Business with LinkedIn*;

Sue Hope, founder of Notary Assist;

Zion Brock, founder of the Get Known Strategy and the On the Hook Game;

Tyler Botsford, founder of Green Monkey Marketing; and

Patrick, Kurt, Mike, and the entire team at TOMM/Rapid Funnel.

None of this could be possible without your commitment to open communication and a win-win for our Notary community. Thank you for blazing a new trail, one never before seen in our industry—evidence that collaboration of epic scale is not only possible, but extremely powerful.

I can't wait to see where we go next.

ABOUT THE AUTHOR

Bill Soroka has helped thousands of Notaries across the U.S. start and scale their dream business with his best-selling book and podcast, *Sign & Thrive*. Today he helps professional mobile Notaries and loan signing agents stop worrying about oversaturation, rising interest rates, and the dread of possibly having to go back to a J-O-B by teaching them how to build a loyal client base so they can have a thriving business in any economic climate, no matter what.

For more information, please visit www.NotaryCoach.com.

Made in United States
Troutdale, OR
01/02/2024

16623886R00159